MIDSUMMER IGHT'S DREAM

Edited by Linda Buckle
Series editors: Richard Andrews and Vicki Wienand
Founding editor: Rex Gibson

CAMBRIDGE
UNIVERSITY PRESS

University Printing House, Cambridge CB2 8BS, United Kingdom

Cambridge University Press is part of the University of Cambridge.

It furthers the University's mission by disseminating knowledge in the pursuit of education, learning and research at the highest international levels of excellence.

www.cambridge.org
Information on this title: www.cambridge.org/9781107615458

First published 1992
Second edition 2000
Third edition 2005
Fourth edition 2014
4th printing 2015

Printed in Poland by Opolgraf

A catalogue record for this publication is available from the British Library

ISBN 978-1-107-61545-8 Paperback

Cover image: Royal Shakespeare Theatre 2011, © Geraint Lewis

Contents

Introduction

This *A Midsummer Night's Dream* is part of the **Cambridge School Shakespeare** series. Like every other play in the series, it has been specially prepared to help all students in schools and colleges.

The **Cambridge School Shakespeare** *A Midsummer Night's Dream* aims to be different. It invites you to lift the words from the page and to bring the play to life in your classroom, hall or drama studio. Through enjoyable and focused activities, you will increase your understanding of the play. Actors have created their different interpretations of the play over the centuries. Similarly, you are invited to make up your own mind about *A Midsummer Night's Dream*, rather than having someone else's interpretation handed down to you.

Cambridge School Shakespeare does not offer you a cut-down or simplified version of the play. This is Shakespeare's language, filled with imaginative possibilities. You will find on every left-hand page: a summary of the action, an explanation of unfamiliar words, and a choice of activities on Shakespeare's stagecraft, characters, themes and language.

Between each act, and in the pages at the end of the play, you will find notes, illustrations and activities. These will help to encourage reflection after every act and give you insights into the background and context of the play as a whole.

This edition will be of value to you whether you are studying for an examination, reading for pleasure or thinking of putting on the play to entertain others. You can work on the activities on your own or in groups. Many of the activities suggest a particular group size, but don't be afraid to make up larger or smaller groups to suit your own purposes. Please don't think you have to do every activity: choose those that will help you most.

Although you are invited to treat *A Midsummer Night's Dream* as a play, you don't need special dramatic or theatrical skills to do the activities. By choosing your activities, and by exploring and experimenting, you can make your own interpretations of Shakespeare's language, characters and stories.

Whatever you do, remember that Shakespeare wrote his plays to be acted, watched and enjoyed.

Rex Gibson
Founding editor

This new edition contains more photographs, more diversity and more supporting material than previous editions, whilst remaining true to Rex's original vision. Specifically, it contains more activities and commentary on stagecraft and writing about Shakespeare, to reflect contemporary interest. The glossary has been enlarged, too. Finally, this edition aims to reflect the best teaching and learning possible, and to represent not only Shakespeare through the ages, but also the relevance and excitement of Shakespeare today.

Richard Andrews and Vicki Wienand
Series editors

This edition of *A Midsummer Night's Dream* uses the text of the play established by R.A. Foakes in **The New Cambridge Shakespeare**.

Theseus, Duke of Athens, and Hippolyta, Queen of the Amazons, are anticipating their wedding. Their plans are interrupted by Egeus, who is having a problem with his daughter, Hermia. Egeus wants to marry Hermia to Demetrius, but she is not co-operating because she is in love with Lysander. Egeus appeals to the duke to support him with a legal judgment, and Theseus decides that Hermia must abide by her father's wishes. Her punishment for disobedience will be a death sentence or a lifetime spent in a nunnery.

The 'course of true love never did run smooth'. Lysander and Hermia plan to avoid the harsh Athenian law and meet in the wood at night, then to elope and marry. Will this solve the problem, or will the jealousy of Demetrius and his ex-love Helena, who plan to follow them, spoil everything?

▼ 'Ill met by moonlight, proud Titania!' The wood is the domain of the fairies, ruled by Oberon and Titania. These powerful beings are in conflict over a changeling boy whom they both wish to have in their service. Their power struggles have reached a critical point, causing a deep rift in their relationship and in the natural world.

▲ The Mechanicals, a group of working men, are rehearsing a play in the wood that night. Their dramatics are decidedly amateur and Puck, Oberon's meddlesome fairy servant, does not think much of them: 'What hempen homespuns have we swaggering here?' Puck mischievously puts an ass's head on Bottom, the individual with the most bravado.

◄ Oberon plans to use a magic love potion on Titania as revenge and to make her more compliant. The potion will 'make or man or woman madly dote / Upon the next live creature that it sees'. By this time, the mortal lovers have all arrived in the forest and Oberon has overheard the discord between Helena and Demetrius. Oberon involves Puck in his plan to resolve the lovers' problems.

Newly transformed into an ass and alone in the forest, Bottom sings to raise his spirits. His awful voice wakes Titania, who immediately falls in love with him: 'O, how I love thee! How I dote on thee!'

▲ In attempting to sort out the lovers' tangle with the magic potion, Puck inadvertently makes things worse. Under the influence of the potion, Lysander abandons Hermia and transfers his affections to Helena. Scenes of jealousy, abuse and rage ensue.

▼ 'Lord, what fools these mortals be!' Directors often make the most of the confusion, anger and hurt to present a crazy world in which love has gone badly wrong.

▼ Puck has been instructed by Oberon to put things right with the four lovers, and all their love problems are magically resolved. 'Are you sure / That we are awake? It seems to me / That yet we sleep, we dream.' Hermia and Lysander, Demetrius and Helena, Theseus and Hippolyta all express confusion about the nature of dreams and reality. However, all are to marry and be happy.

▼ 'My Oberon, what visions have I seen!' Titania is awakened by Oberon as he administers a 'herb' on her eyes and she is able to 'See as thou wast want to see.' She looks with horror on the ass she was 'enamoured of' and is happily united with Oberon in love and harmony.

▼ The Mechanicals perform their play about the tragic love of Pyramus and Thisbe at the wedding, with all the seriousness of amateur theatre. To some extent their play is a parody of the problems faced by the young lovers. Their performance is comic, sad and surreal, providing an opportunity for slapstick humour. Fantasy and reality continue to merge as the theatre audience observes the onstage audience watching the comic performance.

▼ 'This is the silliest stuff that I ever heard.' The audience of newlywed lovers watch the Mechanicals' performance, wide eyed with disbelief.

▼ The performance over, the three couples retire to bed at the end of their wedding day. Oberon and Titania and their attendants arrive to bless the couples with loving marriages and perfect children: 'To the best bride-bed will we, / Which by us shall blessèd be'.

▼ Shakespeare gives Puck the final word. He asks the audience for a round of applause: 'Give me your hands, if we be friends, / And Robin shall restore amends.'

List of characters

The court

HIPPOLYTA Queen of the Amazons, engaged to Theseus
THESEUS Duke of Athens, engaged to Hippolyta
EGEUS father of Hermia
PHILOSTRATE master of the revels to the Athenian court

The lovers

HERMIA in love with Lysander
HELENA in love with Demetrius
LYSANDER in love with Hermia
DEMETRIUS Egeus's choice as a husband for Hermia

The Mechanicals

(workers who put on a play)

NICK BOTTOM a weaver who plays Pyramus
PETER QUINCE a carpenter who speaks the Prologue
FRANCIS FLUTE a bellows-mender who plays Thisbe
TOM SNOUT a tinker who plays Wall
ROBIN STARVELING a tailor who plays Moonshine
SNUG a joiner who plays Lion

The fairies

PUCK (or Robin Goodfellow) Oberon's attendant
OBERON King of the Fairies
TITANIA Queen of the Fairies
PEASEBLOSSOM, COBWEB, MOTH, MUSTARDSEED } Titania's fairy attendants
A FAIRY in Titania's service

Hippolyta and Theseus have been at war and are now to marry to cement the new peace. Theseus regrets that time is moving slowly before he can marry Hippolyta, and orders preparations for their wedding.

Stagecraft

Theseus and Hippolyta

Shakespeare chooses to use two characters from a myth that was well known in his day. Theseus, Duke of Athens, fought a battle with the Amazons (a group of warrior women) and then married Hippolyta, their queen. The opening scene of the play is set in Athens, in Theseus's palace.

Imagine you are planning to direct a performance of *A Midsummer Night's Dream.* Start your own Director's Journal and record your ideas as you go through the play. For this opening scene, consider the following questions:

- How do you want the stage to look as the curtain rises and members of the audience get their first glimpse of this world?
- How would you position your two actors? Think about their relationship, their past and the impact you want their first appearance to have on the audience.

1 Key words and images **(in pairs)**

Write down key words and images in lines 1–19 and look for patterns (such as those to do with the moon, or 'slow' versus 'quickly'). These patterns and the discussion between Theseus and Hippolyta give an idea of what the play is about.

a Make a list of what you consider to be the three most important words or phrases that Theseus uses, while your partner chooses Hippolyta's key words or phrases. Share your ideas and then write a few sentences describing what they reveal about the characters and their situation.

b With your partner, try to predict what might happen in the play. Consider how **imagery** and **symbolism** (see pp. 162–4) could foreshadow events.

Write about it

The moon, the night and dreams

Think about the title of the play and the focus on the moon, night and dreams in the opening speeches. Write two or three paragraphs on the emotions, associations and ideas that this imagery evokes for you.

nuptial hour wedding time

Draws on apace will arrive quickly

step-dame stepmother

dowager widow with money or property

revenue wealth

steep swallow, absorb

solemnities formal ceremonies

pert cheerful, lively

pale companion moon

I wooed thee I tried to win you

pomp celebration

triumph public festivities

revelling merry-making

A Midsummer Night's Dream

Act 1 Scene 1
Athens Theseus' palace

Enter THESEUS, HIPPOLYTA, PHILOSTRATE, *with others.*

THESEUS Now, fair Hippolyta, our nuptial hour
Draws on apace; four happy days bring in
Another moon – but O, methinks, how slow
This old moon wanes! She lingers my desires,
Like to a step-dame or a dowager
Long withering out a young man's revenue.

HIPPOLYTA Four days will quickly steep themselves in night;
Four nights will quickly dream away the time;
And then the moon, like to a silver bow
New bent in heaven, shall behold the night
Of our solemnities.

THESEUS Go, Philostrate,
Stir up the Athenian youth to merriments,
Awake the pert and nimble spirit of mirth;
Turn melancholy forth to funerals;
The pale companion is not for our pomp.
[*Exit Philostrate*]
Hippolyta, I wooed thee with my sword,
And won thy love doing thee injuries;
But I will wed thee in another key,
With pomp, with triumph, and with revelling.

Egeus enters with his daughter Hermia and her two suitors, Lysander (whom she loves) and Demetrius (whom she dislikes). He appeals to Theseus to support his right to decide between them.

1 What kind of father? (in fours)

Is Egeus being totally unreasonable, or is he a responsible Athenian father who is justifiably taking control of Hermia's future and choices? Let one member of your group become Egeus, and the others form a 'court' of justice. Each member of the 'court' prepares one question to ask Egeus, who can then defend and explain himself.

▶ Hippolyta listens intently to Egeus's complaint and watches Hermia's response; she does not speak, but her face is expressive. What might she be thinking? Prepare her thoughts in note form. Then practise these ideas as a monologue. Try voicing them in character to the class.

Language in the play

Language of love (in pairs)

Egeus uses very different language from Theseus and Hippolyta to present love. In pairs, pick out five words that show his attitudes and describe an alternative picture of love from that painted by Hippolyta and Theseus at the start of the scene.

renownèd well known, distinguished

feigning untrue, deceitful

stolen … fantasy stirred her imagination

gauds, conceits fancy trinkets

Knacks knick-knacks

nosegays posies of flowers

sweetmeats sweets, candies

prevailment pressure

filched stolen

Be it so if it turns out that

Enter EGEUS *and his daughter* HERMIA, LYSANDER *and* DEMETRIUS.

EGEUS Happy be Theseus, our renownèd Duke!
THESEUS Thanks, good Egeus. What's the news with thee?
EGEUS Full of vexation come I, with complaint
Against my child, my daughter Hermia.
Stand forth, Demetrius! – My noble lord,
This man hath my consent to marry her.
Stand forth, Lysander! – And, my gracious Duke,
This man hath bewitched the bosom of my child.
Thou, thou, Lysander, thou hast given her rhymes,
And interchanged love-tokens with my child.
Thou hast by moonlight at her window sung
With feigning voice verses of feigning love,
And stolen the impression of her fantasy,
With bracelets of thy hair, rings, gauds, conceits,
Knacks, trifles, nosegays, sweetmeats – messengers
Of strong prevailment in unhardened youth;
With cunning hast thou filched my daughter's heart,
Turned her obedience, which is due to me,
To stubborn harshness. And, my gracious Duke,
Be it so she will not here, before your grace,
Consent to marry with Demetrius,
I beg the ancient privilege of Athens;
As she is mine, I may dispose of her;
Which shall be either to this gentleman
Or to her death, according to our law
Immediately provided in that case.

Hermia pleads to be allowed to choose Lysander for a husband. Theseus warns her to abide by Egeus's decision, otherwise she risks being sent to a convent or to her death.

Themes

Gender and power (in pairs)

The themes of conflict, power and gender are beginning to emerge.

a Who is the most powerful character at this point in the play? Where do our sympathies lie, and why?

b In what ways would life for men and women, and the nature of their relationship, have been different in 1594 (when this play was written) from today? With a partner, draw up a list of your ideas and consider if Shakespeare's contemporaries would have approved of Hermia's confidence in the defence of her choice. Be prepared to share your ideas with the class.

1 Sisterhood

Hermia stands up for herself as a lone female figure, surrounded by squabbling men. Yet she is not alone: Hippolyta, the other female on the stage, says nothing. Why? What is she thinking? Shakespeare has decided to leave her silent. As director, would you have some recognition pass between Hermia and Hippolyta? If so, suggest how it would be done.

Language in the play

Close analysis

HERMIA *I would my father looked but with my eyes.*
THESEUS *Rather your eyes must with his judgement look.*

Write out these quotations at the centre of a blank sheet of paper, and then make brief notes on your analysis of:

- how language is being used
- how character is being developed
- which themes are being explored.

2 Male dominance (in fours)

Already there has been a 'forced' engagement. Go through the play so far, finding any images, **similes** and **metaphors** (see p. 164) that imply male dominance – for example, 'your father should be as a god' (line 47). Read the images about males, then those about females, and say which you find acceptable and which you find offensive – and why.

imprinted moulded, stamped

wanting not having

beseech implore, entreat

abjure reject

blood feelings

livery clothes
aye ever
cloister walkway in a nunnery
mewed confined
barren sister nun

distilled made into perfume

unwishèd yoke unwanted constraint
sovereignty power, control

THESEUS What say you, Hermia? Be advised, fair maid.
To you your father should be as a god,
One that composed your beauties; yea, and one
To whom you are but as a form in wax
By him imprinted, and within his power
To leave the figure, or disfigure it.
Demetrius is a worthy gentleman.
HERMIA So is Lysander.
THESEUS In himself he is;
But in this kind, wanting your father's voice,
The other must be held the worthier.
HERMIA I would my father looked but with my eyes.
THESEUS Rather your eyes must with his judgement look.
HERMIA I do entreat your grace to pardon me.
I know not by what power I am made bold,
Nor how it may concern my modesty
In such a presence here to plead my thoughts;
But I beseech your grace that I may know
The worst that may befall me in this case,
If I refuse to wed Demetrius.
THESEUS Either to die the death, or to abjure
For ever the society of men.
Therefore, fair Hermia, question your desires,
Know of your youth, examine well your blood,
Whether, if you yield not to your father's choice,
You can endure the livery of a nun,
For aye to be in shady cloister mewed,
To live a barren sister all your life,
Chanting faint hymns to the cold fruitless moon.
Thrice blessèd they that master so their blood
To undergo such maiden pilgrimage;
But earthlier happy is the rose distilled
Than that which, withering on the virgin thorn,
Grows, lives, and dies in single blessedness.
HERMIA So will I grow, so live, so die, my lord,
Ere I will yield my virgin patent up
Unto his lordship, whose unwishèd yoke
My soul consents not to give sovereignty.

Theseus orders Hermia to make her decision before his wedding to Hippolyta. Lysander argues his case and points out that Demetrius loved Helena before Hermia, and that Helena still loves Demetrius.

1 Hermia's dilemma – what would you do? (in pairs)

Would you rather die or be imprisoned than marry someone you disliked? (Assume there is no possibility of divorce.) Give reasons for your reply. Make notes on your ideas and then write them up as a paragraph of structured argument. Share your paragraph with a partner.

Themes

Reality and illusion (in pairs)

When Hermia says 'I would my father looked but with my eyes' (line 56), she means that she wishes Egeus could 'see' Lysander as she sees him. The people watching 'see' the debates in this scene very differently.

One of you makes notes about where the sympathies of a Shakespearean audience might lie in this situation. The other makes notes on where a modern audience's sympathies may be. Compare your notes and discuss the different perspectives.

2 'Love' and 'dote' (in small groups)

There has been a good deal of talk about feelings. Talk with your group about which characters are sensitive to others' feelings, and which are not. Compile a list of all the words and phrases so far that describe or explore emotion.

Characters

Lysander

Lysander is beginning to emerge as an interesting character. Consider his response to Demetrius in lines 93–4:

You have her father's love, Demetrius;
Let me have Hermia's – do you marry him.

How do these lines help us to understand Lysander's character? How would you advise an actor to play them? Write some briefing ideas for an actor who has been cast in the role of Lysander. (For more information on Lysander, see p. 160.)

sealing-day wedding day

betwixt between

Diana (Diana was goddess of the moon and of hunting, and she is closely associated with chastity)

austerity self-control, abstinence

crazèd title ridiculous claim

estate unto give to

as well-derived of as good a family and background

well-possessed rich

with vantage rather better

avouch guarantee, swear

to his head to his face

spotted stained unclean (morally)

THESEUS Take time to pause, and by the next new moon,
The sealing-day betwixt my love and me
For everlasting bond of fellowship,
Upon that day either prepare to die
For disobedience to your father's will,
Or else to wed Demetrius, as he would,
Or on Diana's altar to protest
For aye austerity and single life.

DEMETRIUS Relent, sweet Hermia; and, Lysander, yield
Thy crazèd title to my certain right.

LYSANDER You have her father's love, Demetrius;
Let me have Hermia's – do you marry him.

EGEUS Scornful Lysander, true, he hath my love,
And what is mine my love shall render him;
And she is mine, and all my right of her
I do estate unto Demetrius.

LYSANDER I am, my lord, as well-derived as he,
As well-possessed: my love is more than his,
My fortunes every way as fairly ranked,
If not with vantage, as Demetrius';
And, which is more than all these boasts can be,
I am beloved of beauteous Hermia.
Why should not I then prosecute my right?
Demetrius, I'll avouch it to his head,
Made love to Nedar's daughter, Helena,
And won her soul; and she, sweet lady, dotes,
Devoutly dotes, dotes in idolatry,
Upon this spotted and inconstant man.

With a final warning to Hermia, Theseus takes Demetrius and Egeus away to talk to them. Left alone, Lysander and Hermia lament the problems of lovers.

Language in the play

Love, 'short as any dream' (whole class)

a In lines 141–9, Lysander paints love as a temporary thing: 'momentany' (momentary), 'Swift', 'short', 'Brief', surrounded by a hostile world. Talk about what he compares love to, and whether you think the comparisons are suitable.

b Lysander connects love with sinister imagery of 'collied night' and 'the jaws of darkness'. Why do you think this is? He is, after all, a man in love. Do you agree with him? Does love always have a shadowy, dark side? Reflect on your response to these questions. Make brief notes and then share your ideas in a class discussion.

Themes

'The course of true love never did run smooth' (in small groups)

Line 134 has become a commonplace saying. How true is it? Think about what it might suggest about the rest of the play. Make a list of movies, novels, poems and TV series that explore this theme. Then update your list with ideas from everyone in your group. See which group in the class can compile the longest list.

1 The dance of the lovers – who loves whom? (I)

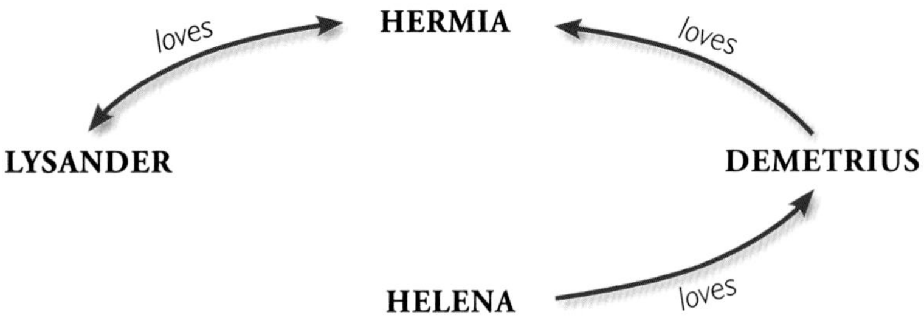

▲ **Discuss this diagram with a partner, then individually write a brief description of what it shows.**

fancies desires
yields you up gives you up
extenuate change, reduce

what cheer how are you

Against in preparation for

Belike probably
Beteem grant
tempest of my eyes stormy tears
aught anything

blood class, family background
enthralled bound
misgraffèd mismatched

momentany momentary

collied darkened, like coal
spleen burst of temper

THESEUS I must confess that I have heard so much,
And with Demetrius thought to have spoke thereof;
But, being overfull of self-affairs,
My mind did lose it. But Demetrius, come,
And come, Egeus. You shall go with me;
I have some private schooling for you both.
For you, fair Hermia, look you arm yourself
To fit your fancies to your father's will;
Or else the law of Athens yields you up
(Which by no means we may extenuate)
To death, or to a vow of single life.
Come, my Hippolyta; what cheer, my love?
Demetrius and Egeus, go along;
I must employ you in some business
Against our nuptial, and confer with you
Of something nearly that concerns yourselves.

EGEUS With duty and desire we follow you.

Exeunt all but Lysander and Hermia

LYSANDER How now, my love? Why is your cheek so pale?
How chance the roses there do fade so fast?

HERMIA Belike for want of rain, which I could well
Beteem them from the tempest of my eyes.

LYSANDER Ay me! For aught that I could ever read,
Could ever hear by tale or history,
The course of true love never did run smooth;
But either it was different in blood –

HERMIA O cross! too high to be enthralled to low.

LYSANDER Or else misgraffèd in respect of years –

HERMIA O spite! too old to be engaged to young.

LYSANDER Or else it stood upon the choice of friends –

HERMIA O hell, to choose love by another's eyes!

LYSANDER Or, if there were a sympathy in choice,
War, death, or sickness did lay siege to it,
Making it momentany as a sound,
Swift as a shadow, short as any dream,
Brief as the lightning in the collied night,
That in a spleen unfolds both heaven and earth,
And, ere a man hath power to say 'Behold!',
The jaws of darkness do devour it up.
So quick bright things come to confusion.

Lysander and Hermia plan to elope: to run away to Lysander's widowed aunt who lives beyond the reach of the Athenian law. They arrange to meet 'tomorrow night' in the wood outside the city.

crossed thwarted, frustrated

edict command

fancy's love's

persuasion doctrine, set of principles

leagues (a league is about three miles)

respects me regards me

without outside

do observance celebrate

simplicity openness and sincerity

doves (they represent love and faithfulness)

1 How old? (in threes)

Because of their behaviour, perhaps Shakespeare is suggesting that the lovers are very young (remember that Juliet in *Romeo and Juliet* was not quite fourteen). Suggest how old you think Hermia, Lysander and Demetrius are. Consequently, how old are Theseus and Hippolyta? Give reasons for your opinions.

Language in the play

What do lovers dream? (in pairs)

Hermia speaks of features of love ('fancy's followers') such as thoughts and wishes and dreams. Talk with a partner about what sort of dreams lovers have (being together, freedom from restrictions, happiness, sex, and so on). Hermia also swears oaths by the goddess of love (Venus) and other lovers (Dido, Queen of Carthage, who loved Aeneas, the false Trojan). For Hermia, love is like a dream in which she lives all the time. With your partner, analyse your favourite quotation from Hermia on this page. Then write down your ideas about the following questions:

- Is this what love is like?
- Are people who are in love inhabiting a dream world?
- Is love a fantasy or a reality?

Share your ideas with another pair.

HERMIA If then true lovers have been ever crossed
It stands as an edict in destiny.
Then let us teach our trial patience,
Because it is a customary cross,
As due to love as thoughts, and dreams, and sighs,
Wishes, and tears – poor fancy's followers.

LYSANDER A good persuasion. Therefore hear me, Hermia:
I have a widow aunt, a dowager,
Of great revenue, and she hath no child.
From Athens is her house remote seven leagues;
And she respects me as her only son.
There, gentle Hermia, may I marry thee;
And to that place the sharp Athenian law
Cannot pursue us. If thou lov'st me, then
Steal forth thy father's house tomorrow night,
And in the wood, a league without the town
(Where I did meet thee once with Helena
To do observance to a morn of May),
There will I stay for thee.

HERMIA My good Lysander,
I swear to thee by Cupid's strongest bow,
By his best arrow with the golden head,
By the simplicity of Venus' doves,
By that which knitteth souls and prospers loves,
And by that fire which burned the Carthage queen
When the false Trojan under sail was seen,
By all the vows that ever men have broke
(In number more than ever women spoke),
In that same place thou hast appointed me,
Tomorrow truly will I meet with thee.

LYSANDER Keep promise, love. Look, here comes Helena.

Helena enters and talks of Demetrius's love for Hermia. She wishes she were like Hermia. To console her, Hermia and Lysander tell her of their plan to elope.

1 What do you make of Helena? (in pairs)

a Read through Helena's and Hermia's lines 180–207, then identify key words and phrases that reveal Helena's character. Act out the dialogue with your partner, emphasising those key words and phrases.

b What is your first impression of Helena? From her opening speeches, describe her character in three words.

2 How might it end?

Shakespeare has set up an extremely difficult situation for his lovers (remember that Helena is in love too, though it is unrequited). If the play is a Shakespearean comedy, in the sense that there is a happy ending for all the lovers (see p. 150), it's difficult to see how the situation will be resolved. Invent a plotline that might bring all the couples together at the end.

Language in the play

Patterns of language

Look at the 'Language' section on pages 162–5, which describes some of the language features in the play. Use this information to write notes on the patterns of language in lines 180–207. Consider the effects of **blank verse**, imagery, simile and metaphor. Find examples of devices such as repetition of words or sounds, **juxtapositions** (the placement of contrasting words or ideas next to each other), romantic **diction** (choice of words) and classical **allusions** (see p. 153). What do these patterns suggest about the relationship between Helena and Hermia?

Themes

Change and translation

Shakespeare introduces the theme of change and the idea of being 'translated' when (in lines 192–3) Helena pleads with Hermia to:

teach me how you look, and with what art
You sway the motion of Demetrius' heart.

This becomes an increasingly important theme, so look out for further exploration of these ideas as you progress through the play. Have there been any changes or translations already?

Whither away? where are you going?

fair beautiful

lodestars guiding stars

favour appearance

tongue's sweet melody voice

bated excepted

Phoebe Diana, goddess of the moon, (see p. 8)

visage face

Enter HELENA.

HERMIA God speed, fair Helena! Whither away?
HELENA Call you me fair? That 'fair' again unsay.
Demetrius loves your fair: O happy fair!
Your eyes are lodestars, and your tongue's sweet air
More tuneable than lark to shepherd's ear
When wheat is green, when hawthorn buds appear.
Sickness is catching. O, were favour so,
Yours would I catch, fair Hermia, ere I go;
My ear should catch your voice, my eye your eye,
My tongue should catch your tongue's sweet melody.
Were the world mine, Demetrius being bated,
The rest I'd give to be to you translated.
O, teach me how you look, and with what art
You sway the motion of Demetrius' heart.
HERMIA I frown upon him; yet he loves me still.
HELENA O that your frowns would teach my smiles such skill!
HERMIA I give him curses; yet he gives me love.
HELENA O that my prayers could such affection move!
HERMIA The more I hate, the more he follows me.
HELENA The more I love, the more he hateth me.
HERMIA His folly, Helena, is no fault of mine.
HELENA None but your beauty; would that fault were mine!
HERMIA Take comfort: he no more shall see my face;
Lysander and myself will fly this place.
Before the time I did Lysander see,
Seemed Athens as a paradise to me.
O then, what graces in my love do dwell,
That he hath turned a heaven unto a hell?
LYSANDER Helen, to you our minds we will unfold:
Tomorrow night, when Phoebe doth behold
Her silver visage in the watery glass,
Decking with liquid pearl the bladed grass
(A time that lovers' flights doth still conceal),
Through Athens' gates have we devised to steal.

Hermia and Lysander leave, wishing Helena luck with Demetrius. Helena reflects on the transforming and deceiving nature of love, and decides to tell Demetrius of the elopement in order to win his thanks.

Write about it

Your view of the lovers (in fours)

Each group member chooses one of the four lovers.

a Individually, write a paragraph on your character, analysing what you consider to be their most important or powerful quotation so far. In turn, read your paragraphs aloud to your group.

b Together, reach a consensus. How are the lovers different or similar? Which one do you like best (and least)? Who speaks most convincingly about love? Share the group's consensus with the class.

1 Love – 'winged Cupid' – Helena's view

(in small groups)

Helena explains what she thinks of love in lines 232–9, using the comparison of Cupid (the mythical god of love, a young child with wings, who was sometimes presented as being blind).

Helena says, in lines 234–5:

Love looks not with the eyes, but with the mind,
And therefore is winged Cupid painted blind.

Shakespeare is exploring some interesting and complex ideas here in relation to love. Why do you think Cupid has become a symbol of love? Is the mind more important than the eyes when in love? In what ways could love be said to make a person blind? Talk about these questions with your group in preparation for a class discussion.

were wont used

counsel sweet friendly advice

Keep word keep your word, be loyal

adieu farewell

holding no quantity having no value

figure suggest

beguiled tricked

waggish mischievous

game sport

forswear falsely promise

perjured deliberately misled

ere before

eyne eyes

intelligence information

dear expense great sacrifice

HERMIA And in the wood, where often you and I
Upon faint primrose beds were wont to lie,
Emptying our bosoms of their counsel sweet,
There my Lysander and myself shall meet,
And thence from Athens turn away our eyes
To seek new friends and stranger companies.
Farewell, sweet playfellow; pray thou for us,
And good luck grant thee thy Demetrius.
Keep word, Lysander; we must starve our sight
From lovers' food till morrow deep midnight.

LYSANDER I will, my Hermia.

Exit Hermia

Helena, adieu!
As you on him, Demetrius dote on you. *Exit Lysander*

HELENA How happy some o'er other some can be!
Through Athens I am thought as fair as she.
But what of that? Demetrius thinks not so;
He will not know what all but he do know.
And as he errs, doting on Hermia's eyes,
So I, admiring of his qualities.
Things base and vile, holding no quantity,
Love can transpose to form and dignity.
Love looks not with the eyes, but with the mind,
And therefore is winged Cupid painted blind.
Nor hath love's mind of any judgement taste;
Wings, and no eyes, figure unheedy haste;
And therefore is love said to be a child
Because in choice he is so oft beguiled.
As waggish boys in game themselves forswear,
So the boy Love is perjured everywhere;
For, ere Demetrius looked on Hermia's eyne,
He hailed down oaths that he was only mine,
And when this hail some heat from Hermia felt,
So he dissolved, and showers of oaths did melt.
I will go tell him of fair Hermia's flight:
Then to the wood will he, tomorrow night,
Pursue her; and for this intelligence,
If I have thanks it is a dear expense;
But herein mean I to enrich my pain,
To have his sight thither, and back again. *Exit*

A group of workers (the Mechanicals) – Quince, Snug, Bottom, Flute, Snout and Starveling – meet to allocate the parts for a play, which they hope to perform at Duke Theseus's wedding.

1 Who have we here? (in sixes)

To gain an impression of the Mechanicals, take a character each and act out the whole scene. Then work on one or both of the following activities.

Characters

The Mechanicals (in sixes)

Shakespeare gives these characters distinctive names and trades. Consider how the name and trade of each helps establish character. Choose a character and work for a little while on your own, reading your character's lines and thinking about how to develop your part. Come back together in your group to act out this scene again.

Stagecraft

The court and the workmen (in small groups)

The Mechanicals provide a real contrast with the mythical court of Athens, if only because they are so clearly of Shakespeare's time and place.

a In your group, talk about the differences between the court and the workmen, and why Shakespeare might have included the Mechanicals and their very different world.

b How could you reveal this different world on stage? Consider the choices a set and costume designer, a lighting engineer and an actor might make. Write your ideas in your Director's Journal.

scrip script

interlude play

treats on is about

grow to a point come to the point

Marry by the Virgin Mary (a mild oath)

lamentable sad, distressing

Pyramus and Thisbe two characters from Roman mythology who had an ill-fated romance

spread yourselves spread out

condole show grief

chief humour main preference

Ercles Hercules

to tear a cat in to rant and rave (what type of acting is Bottom used to, and what type of play?)

Phibbus Phoebus, god of the sun, who was believed to drive a chariot ('car') through the sky

mar tarnish, spoil

Act 1 Scene 2
Athens

Enter QUINCE *the Carpenter, and* SNUG *the Joiner, and* BOTTOM *the Weaver, and* FLUTE *the Bellows-mender, and* SNOUT *the Tinker and* STARVELING *the Tailor.*

QUINCE Is all our company here?

BOTTOM You were best to call them generally, man by man, according to the scrip.

QUINCE Here is the scroll of every man's name which is thought fit through all Athens to play in our interlude before the Duke and the Duchess on his wedding day at night.

BOTTOM First, good Peter Quince, say what the play treats on; then read the names of the actors; and so grow to a point.

QUINCE Marry, our play is 'The most lamentable comedy and most cruel death of Pyramus and Thisbe'.

BOTTOM A very good piece of work, I assure you, and a merry. Now, good Peter Quince, call forth your actors by the scroll. Masters, spread yourselves.

QUINCE Answer as I call you. Nick Bottom, the weaver?

BOTTOM Ready. Name what part I am for, and proceed.

QUINCE You, Nick Bottom, are set down for Pyramus.

BOTTOM What is Pyramus? A lover or a tyrant?

QUINCE A lover that kills himself, most gallant, for love.

BOTTOM That will ask some tears in the true performing of it. If I do it, let the audience look to their eyes: I will move storms, I will condole, in some measure. To the rest – yet my chief humour is for a tyrant. I could play Ercles rarely, or a part to tear a cat in, to make all split:

The raging rocks
And shivering shocks
Shall break the locks
  Of prison gates,
And Phibbus' car
Shall shine from far,
And make and mar
  The foolish Fates.

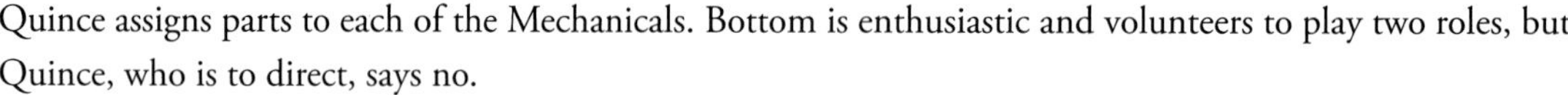
Quince assigns parts to each of the Mechanicals. Bottom is enthusiastic and volunteers to play two roles, but Quince, who is to direct, says no.

Stagecraft

Physical and verbal humour (in pairs)

How would you direct this scene to make the most of the comic opportunities? Consider the following:

- **'a monstrous little voice'** The problem of Flute playing a woman (lines 36–44) is partly solved, so the Mechanicals believe, by Flute speaking in a high-pitched voice. How could voice, manner and gesture produce comedy?
- **'let not me play a woman'** On Shakespeare's stage, all the actors were male. How could you make the most of the comic value of a man playing a woman?
- **'I have a beard coming'** Flute could be played by a young actor who has not yet started shaving, or an actor with a beard who is using this excuse to avoid playing the part. Consider which would be the most amusing for the audience. Do you have any other suggestions on how to make this line funny?
- **'they would shriek'** The Mechanicals seem to think that if Bottom played the lion's part he would frighten the women in the audience. They clearly have very little experience of acting. Suggest how you would make their amateur attempts humorous.

Write your ideas on all these points in your Director's Journal.

Themes

More transformations (in fours)

The Mechanicals are attempting to transform themselves into actors playing classical characters. Flute has to pretend to be a woman. This is very much a play about change. For the audience, Shakespeare has transformed the setting from a court, with a duke and a queen, into a wood with a comical group of workers.

a Speak the Mechanicals' dialogue in a way that will highlight this change. For example, you could experiment with different accents. The Mechanicals' lines are written in prose and the court speeches in poetry. How would this sound different for the audience? Again, play with tone and emphasis.

b Watch out for more transformations as the play progresses, and make a note of each one you spot.

Ercles' vein Hercules's style

condoling comforting

small high pitched

fitted cast

This was lofty. Now name the rest of the players. – This is Ercles' vein, a tyrant's vein; a lover is more condoling.

QUINCE Francis Flute, the bellows-mender?

FLUTE Here, Peter Quince.

QUINCE Flute, you must take Thisbe on you.

FLUTE What is Thisbe? A wandering knight?

QUINCE It is the lady that Pyramus must love.

FLUTE Nay, faith, let not me play a woman: I have a beard coming.

QUINCE That's all one: you shall play it in a mask, and you may speak as small as you will.

BOTTOM And I may hide my face, let me play Thisbe too. I'll speak in a monstrous little voice: 'Thisne, Thisne!' – 'Ah, Pyramus, my lover dear; thy Thisbe dear, and lady dear.'

QUINCE No, no; you must play Pyramus; and Flute, you Thisbe.

BOTTOM Well, proceed.

QUINCE Robin Starveling, the tailor?

STARVELING Here, Peter Quince.

QUINCE Robin Starveling, you must play Thisbe's mother. Tom Snout, the tinker?

SNOUT Here, Peter Quince.

QUINCE You, Pyramus' father; myself, Thisbe's father; Snug, the joiner, you the lion's part; and I hope here is a play fitted.

Quince completes the arrangements for the play, despite Bottom's interruptions. They plan to meet in the wood 'tomorrow night' for a private rehearsal.

▲ What line might Bottom (in the pink shirt) be speaking here?

Language in the play

The Mechanicals' language

The Mechanicals' language is very different from that of the court characters. Make a list of contradictions, mistakes and odd things they say in Scene 2. Then choose two or three examples of speech from the court characters in Scene 1. Use these quotations as a starting point for an analysis of similarities and differences.

Write about it

A Mechanical's reflection (by yourself)

Imagine you are one of the Mechanicals reflecting on your first rehearsal after you have arrived home. Write a diary account of the rehearsal, the allocation of parts and Bottom's behaviour.

extempore as an ad lib (without advance preparation)

discretion choice

aggravate moderate

proper handsome

French-crown sexually transmitted disease, leading to baldness

con learn

be dogged with company have people watching

draw a bill of properties compile a list of props

be perfect know your lines perfectly

hold … bowstrings keep your word

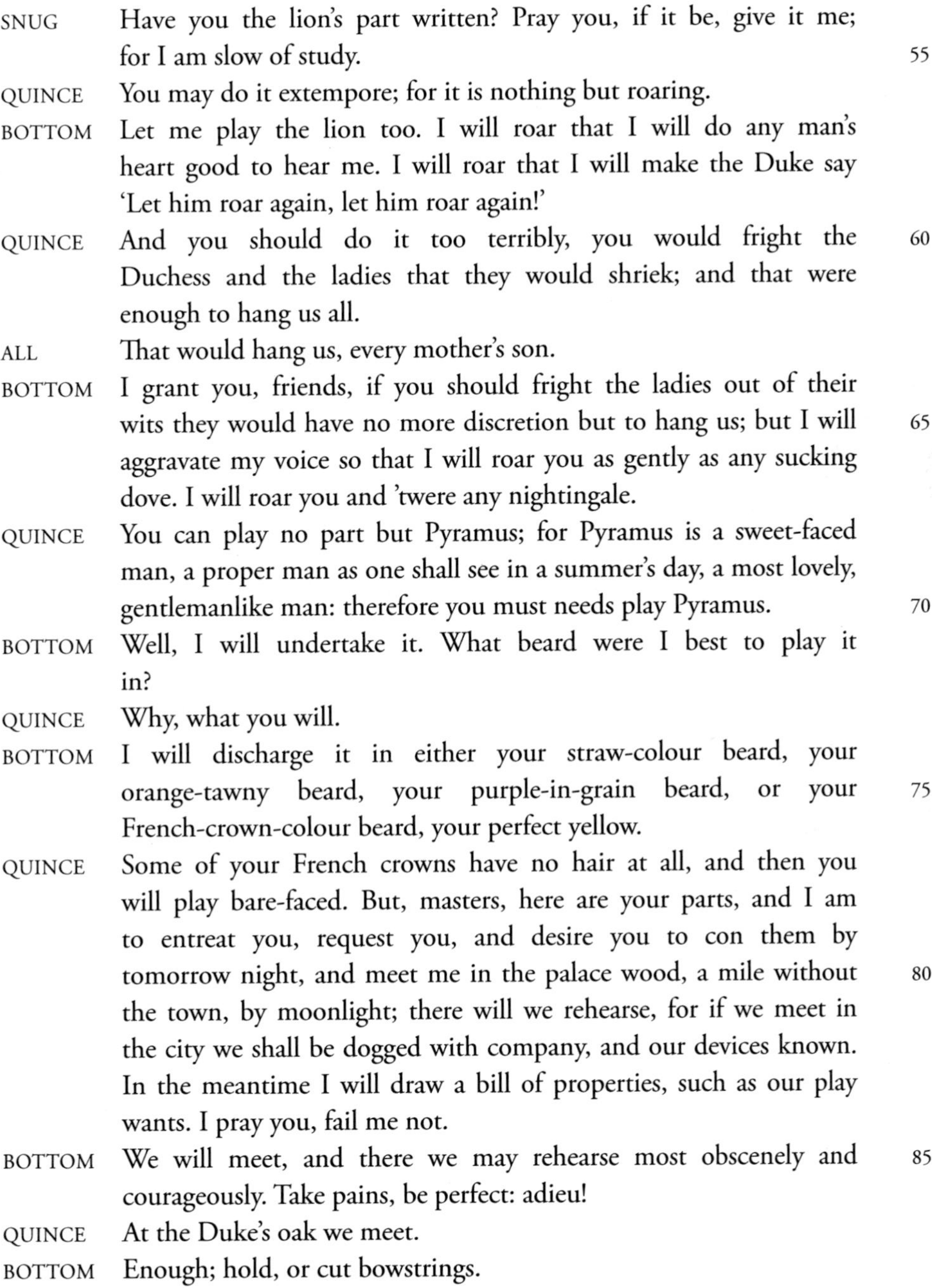

SNUG Have you the lion's part written? Pray you, if it be, give it me; for I am slow of study.

QUINCE You may do it extempore; for it is nothing but roaring.

BOTTOM Let me play the lion too. I will roar that I will do any man's heart good to hear me. I will roar that I will make the Duke say 'Let him roar again, let him roar again!'

QUINCE And you should do it too terribly, you would fright the Duchess and the ladies that they would shriek; and that were enough to hang us all.

ALL That would hang us, every mother's son.

BOTTOM I grant you, friends, if you should fright the ladies out of their wits they would have no more discretion but to hang us; but I will aggravate my voice so that I will roar you as gently as any sucking dove. I will roar you and 'twere any nightingale.

QUINCE You can play no part but Pyramus; for Pyramus is a sweet-faced man, a proper man as one shall see in a summer's day, a most lovely, gentlemanlike man: therefore you must needs play Pyramus.

BOTTOM Well, I will undertake it. What beard were I best to play it in?

QUINCE Why, what you will.

BOTTOM I will discharge it in either your straw-colour beard, your orange-tawny beard, your purple-in-grain beard, or your French-crown-colour beard, your perfect yellow.

QUINCE Some of your French crowns have no hair at all, and then you will play bare-faced. But, masters, here are your parts, and I am to entreat you, request you, and desire you to con them by tomorrow night, and meet me in the palace wood, a mile without the town, by moonlight; there will we rehearse, for if we meet in the city we shall be dogged with company, and our devices known. In the meantime I will draw a bill of properties, such as our play wants. I pray you, fail me not.

BOTTOM We will meet, and there we may rehearse most obscenely and courageously. Take pains, be perfect: adieu!

QUINCE At the Duke's oak we meet.

BOTTOM Enough; hold, or cut bowstrings.

Exeunt

Looking back at Act 1

Activities for groups or individuals

1 Emotional hooks

Look again at the decisions Shakespeare has made for the start of this play. Now that you have finished the first act, consider how his choices engage the audience emotionally with the characters and the action.

- **a** List the decisions Shakespeare makes with regard to setting, staging, introduction of characters and their situation, plot, language and dialogue.
- **b** With each dramatic technique you have listed, decide how successful you think it is at emotionally engaging the audience, and note down the reasons for your decision.

2 Egeus: a bully, or something else?

Egeus may appear simply as an egotistical bully. But he can be played to present a different impression. Explain your opinion of Egeus in three or four sentences.

3 Love

A Midsummer Night's Dream is a play very much about love. Yet in one of the harsher moments in the play, Egeus describes love as 'feigning' and 'cunning' (Act 1 Scene 1, lines 31 and 36).

In pairs, talk together about 'love' and what you think it is. Identify what the play suggests are the problems love can cause and consider what solutions there might be to these problems. Then, with the same partner, improvise a chat-show interview. Partner A plays one of the lovers and Partner B the chat-show host who asks about their relationship, the nature of their love and the problems they are encountering. Partner A answers in role.

4 Hippolyta – and Queen Elizabeth I

The photograph below shows the character of Hippolyta dressed to look like Queen Elizabeth I. Hippolyta is the queen of the Amazons, yet says very little in the play. Elizabeth I chose to remain unmarried and had been queen for over thirty years when *A Midsummer Night's Dream* was written. How do you think the Elizabethan audience would have interpreted the character of Hippolyta? Find a quotation from Act 1 to support your ideas.

5 More history – Bottom's version

The Mechanicals' fear of bringing on a lion may be based on an actual incident. Just before Shakespeare wrote the play, a lion was excluded from celebrations in the Scottish court because it 'might have brought some fear'. The story was well known.

a Imagine Bottom tells that tale to the other Mechanicals. Write him a speech of ten lines – in his own unique style.

b Write about your reaction to this context. What does it add to our understanding of Shakespeare's purpose with Bottom and an Elizabethan audience's response to him?

6 Word pictures – verbal imagery

The words characters speak often create 'word pictures', or images in your mind. Some phrases conjure up clear visual pictures – for example, 'Chanting faint hymns to the cold fruitless moon' (Scene 1, line 73). Other expressions are more complex and are difficult to visualise, such as 'Swift as a shadow, short as any dream' (Scene 1, line 144).

All imagery can contribute a great deal to your imaginative understanding of the play. Identify five images in the first act. Discuss which are visual and which are not.

7 Stage pictures – visual imagery

A play combines verbal imagery with visual images (e.g. the actors' gestures and actions). Sometimes the visual images match the verbal imagery. For example, when Hermia says 'I swear to thee by Cupid's strongest bow, / By his best arrow with the golden head,' (Scene 1, lines 169–70), what gesture might she make to express the image physically?

Pick a short passage with an interesting verbal image from Act 1 and rehearse it with physical actions. You may want to show this performance to the class, or take a photograph and use the verbal image as a caption.

▶ In a 2002 production at Shakespeare's Globe, Snug's mane was made of a bathmat! In what other ways could you use costume and gesture to highlight the comedy of this supposedly terrifying lion?

A fairy in the service of Titania, Queen of the Fairies, meets Puck. Puck explains the conflict over an Indian boy between Oberon, King of the Fairies, and Titania.

Stagecraft

'*Enter a* FAIRY'

One of Shakespeare's favourite dramatic techniques is to contrast one scene with another. Here, after presenting the worlds of the court and the Mechanicals to the audience, he introduces a third world: the fairy kingdom. Try one or both of the following activities to gain a first impression of the fairy world.

a **Mind movie** Relax and close your eyes as your teacher reads the poetry (lines 2–31) aloud to you. Imagine or draw this world as vividly as you can. Share your picture with a partner.

b **Comparisons and contrasts** Compare and contrast this fairy world with the two worlds presented in Act 1. In your Director's Journal draw up a table of the three worlds, like the one below.

Features	The court	The Mechanicals	The fairies
Characters		e.g. Bottom	
Nature of conflicts	e.g. marriage		
Setting			e.g. wood

c Add additional features that it would be useful to compare – for example, the language that is used and the themes that are introduced and explored in each of the three worlds. Decide on the key similarities and differences between the worlds.

Language in the play

What does the audience see? (in pairs)

Both speeches in the script opposite create visions (or dreams) in the audience's mind of things that happen in the fairy world. Some images would be very difficult to put on a stage – for example, 'elves for fear / Creep into acorn cups' (lines 30–1).

Discuss how much help the audience needs to imagine what is described by the actors. Make some suggestions about props, staging, set and how the actors engage with and respond to the language. Write up your suggestions.

whither where

Thorough through

briar thorny bush

pale fence

sphere orbit

orbs fairy rings

cowslips wild flowers that stand upright

pensioners gentlemen of the royal bodyguard who often dressed splendidly in golden uniforms

savours scent

seek some dewdrops … ear (contemporary thought was that pearls originated from dewdrops; pearls were fashionable in Elizabethan earrings, and Shakespeare is making a connection between the royal courts of Elizabeth and the fairy queen)

lob lout

anon soon

revels merry-making

passing … wrath very fierce and angry

changeling human child swapped by fairies for one of their own

Knight of his train an important soldier, one of his attendants

trace wander through

perforce by force

starlight sheen shining starlight

square quarrel

Act 2 Scene 1
The wood

Enter a FAIRY *at one door, and* PUCK, *or* ROBIN GOODFELLOW *at another.*

PUCK How now, spirit; whither wander you?
FAIRY Over hill, over dale,
Thorough bush, thorough briar,
Over park, over pale,
Thorough flood, thorough fire;
I do wander everywhere
Swifter than the moon's sphere;
And I serve the Fairy Queen,
To dew her orbs upon the green.
The cowslips tall her pensioners be;
In their gold coats spots you see –
Those be rubies, fairy favours,
In those freckles live their savours.
I must go seek some dewdrops here,
And hang a pearl in every cowslip's ear.
Farewell, thou lob of spirits; I'll be gone.
Our Queen and all her elves come here anon.
PUCK The King doth keep his revels here tonight.
Take heed the Queen come not within his sight,
For Oberon is passing fell and wrath,
Because that she as her attendant hath
A lovely boy stol'n from an Indian king;
She never had so sweet a changeling,
And jealous Oberon would have the child
Knight of his train, to trace the forests wild
But she perforce withholds the lovèd boy,
Crowns him with flowers, and makes him all her joy.
And now they never meet in grove or green,
By fountain clear or spangled starlight sheen,
But they do square, that all their elves for fear
Creep into acorn cups and hide them there.

Puck and the fairy talk about the sort of 'sprite' Puck is. In both descriptions, he is mischievous and plays tricks.

1 The Cottingley fairies (whole class)

People have long wanted to believe in the existence of fairies. In 1917, two girls took five photographs of themselves with 'fairies' in the woods near their house. For decades, even eminent scientists and scholars believed these to be authentic. In their old age, the two girls finally admitted that the photographs were faked. Debate why you think fairies continue to have such a hold on the imagination.

Write about it

Puck (in pairs)

a Look carefully at the presentations of Puck shown in the images throughout this book (see pp. 36, 68, 96, 142, 146, 148, 149 and 158). Think about costumes, make-up, positioning on stage, body language, facial expression, characterisation and so on. With a partner, discuss the presentations one by one and write down one observation on each.

b Individually, pick one presentation that represents your personal response to Puck. Using this image as a starting point, write one paragraph that analyses how Shakespeare introduces Puck at the start of Act 2, and the initial impact this character has on an audience. Integrate at least three short quotations into your writing.

shrewd evil or mischievous

knavish roguish, unprincipled

sprite spirit

Skim milk skim the cream off the milk so it will not churn into butter

labour in the quern clog up the hand mill for grinding corn

bootless fruitlessly, in vain

barm head (on beer)

jest joke

a fat and bean-fed … foal trick a fat horse by neighing like a filly (young female horse)

gossip's bowl bowl of a tale-telling woman

crab crab apple, often used to flavour beer

dewlap hanging, loose skin on the neck

aunt old woman

for threefoot … topples she mistakes me for a three-legged stool, then I slip from beneath her and she falls down

loffe laugh (here, and with the words 'waxen' and 'neeze', Puck is imitating the rural dialect and accent)

waxen wax, increase, get louder

neeze sneeze

FAIRY Either I mistake your shape and making quite,
Or else you are that shrewd and knavish sprite
Called Robin Goodfellow. Are not you he
That frights the maidens of the villagery,
Skim milk, and sometimes labour in the quern,
And bootless make the breathless housewife churn,
And sometime make the drink to bear no barm,
Mislead night-wanderers, laughing at their harm?
Those that 'Hobgoblin' call you, and 'Sweet Puck',
You do their work, and they shall have good luck.
Are not you he?

PUCK Thou speakest aright;
I am that merry wanderer of the night.
I jest to Oberon, and make him smile
When I a fat and bean-fed horse beguile,
Neighing in likeness of a filly foal;
And sometime lurk I in a gossip's bowl
In very likeness of a roasted crab,
And when she drinks, against her lips I bob,
And on her withered dewlap pour the ale.
The wisest aunt, telling the saddest tale,
Sometime for threefoot stool mistaketh me;
Then slip I from her bum, down topples she,
And 'Tailor' cries, and falls into a cough;
And then the whole choir hold their hips and loffe,
And waxen in their mirth, and neeze, and swear
A merrier hour was never wasted there.
But room, Fairy: here comes Oberon.

FAIRY And here my mistress. Would that he were gone!

Oberon and Titania enter with their attendants. They accuse each other of being attracted to the mortals Theseus and Hippolyta.

Stagecraft

Introducing Titania and Oberon (in pairs)

The entrance of Titania and Oberon, King and Queen of the Fairies, is an important and memorable moment for most audiences. A director has many options for how to introduce these dramatic characters with their attendants.

With your partner, consider the mood and tone of the initial conversation between Titania and Oberon, what it reveals of their relationship and why they are in conflict. Then devise a list of suggestions for the director of a new stage production to consider when introducing these two characters. Think about music, lighting, method of entry, positioning on stage, costume, make-up, props and so on. Write your ideas in your Director's Journal and be prepared to share them with the class.

train attendants, servants of Oberon and Titania

forsworn his bed and company decided not to sleep with him or spend any time with him

Tarry wait

rash wanton thoughtless and wilful creature

lord … lady (they are husband and wife)

Corin … Phillida two mythical lovers; also, traditional names for a shepherd and his wife

pipes of corn (shepherds played music on straws made from plant stems)

forsooth in truth

buskined wearing hunting boots (a reminder of Hippolyta's prowess in hunting)

Glance at my credit attack my reputation

Perigenia … Aegles … Ariadne … Antiopa women Theseus loved and left (another example of Shakespeare weaving myth, legend, classics, history and folklore into the play)

Enter [OBERON,] *the King of Fairies, at one door, with his train; and* [TITANIA,] *the Queen, at another with hers.*

OBERON Ill met by moonlight, proud Titania!
TITANIA What, jealous Oberon? Fairies, skip hence.
I have forsworn his bed and company.
OBERON Tarry, rash wanton! Am not I thy lord?
TITANIA Then I must be thy lady. But I know
When thou hast stol'n away from Fairyland,
And in the shape of Corin sat all day
Playing on pipes of corn, and versing love
To amorous Phillida. Why art thou here
Come from the farthest step of India? –
But that, forsooth, the bouncing Amazon,
Your buskined mistress and your warrior love,
To Theseus must be wedded; and you come
To give their bed joy and prosperity.
OBERON How canst thou thus, for shame, Titania,
Glance at my credit with Hippolyta,
Knowing I know thy love to Theseus?
Didst not thou lead him through the glimmering night
From Perigenia, whom he ravishèd,
And make him with fair Aegles break his faith,
With Ariadne, and Antiopa?

Titania claims that the dispute with Oberon has changed the natural patterns of the climate and the seasons.

Language in the play

Changing world – changing language

Our world is always changing, and so is our language. You can see some of these changes by comparing Shakespeare's words and phrases with the way we speak and write today.

a Use Titania's lines 81–117 to look for evidence of an older way of life ('ox … stretched his yoke') and beliefs ('Contagious fogs'). You can see how writing about an older way of life means using different language.

b Make a list of what we can learn from these lines about the similarities and differences between Elizabethan times and today. Remember, though, that these are fairies talking. Reflect on how Shakespeare is presenting this as an unreal world with magical powers. For example, Titania describes the disruption of the natural world because of the conflict between her and Oberon (this suggests their power in and over nature). Look for other examples and make a note of them.

Write about it

Relationships: fairy world, court world

a Think about the relationship between Titania and Oberon, as shown in lines 60–117, and the sexual nature of their conversation. Write notes on the parallels you see here with the relationships in Act 1.

b What does Titania mean when she says 'These are the forgeries of jealousy' (line 81)? Write two or three paragraphs about power, conflict and jealousy within the relationships in this play. Consider Hippolyta and Theseus, Lysander and Hermia, Demetrius and Helena and Titania and Oberon. Pick two couples to compare and contrast.

forgeries lies

middle summer's spring beginning of midsummer

pavèd flowing over stones or pebbles

beachèd margent shore

ringlets dancing in a circle

brawls quarrels (also a dance)

Contagious fogs fogs that bring disease (Elizabethans believed that disease was carried in the air)

pelting paltry, insignificant

murrion flock diseased sheep

nine-men's-morris outdoor game (like draughts)

quaint mazes mazes made of turf, popular during the Elizabethan age (also refers to Theseus rescuing Ariadne from the Minotaur's maze)

wanton green lush grass

want their winter cheer are unable to enjoy winter amusements

rheumatic diseases (these were linked to the body fluid rheum, from the nose or eyes)

distemperature disorder in the weather and the body

hoary-headed frosts white frost

old Hiems winter personified

odorous chaplet sweet-smelling circlet for the hair

childing pregnant, fruitful

change exchange

wonted liveries usual clothes

mazèd amazed, confused

progeny offspring

debate quarrel

dissension disagreement

TITANIA These are the forgeries of jealousy:
And never since the middle summer's spring
Met we on hill, in dale, forest, or mead,
By pavèd fountain or by rushy brook,
Or in the beachèd margent of the sea
To dance our ringlets to the whistling wind,
But with thy brawls thou hast disturbed our sport.
Therefore the winds, piping to us in vain,
As in revenge have sucked up from the sea
Contagious fogs; which, falling in the land,
Hath every pelting river made so proud
That they have overborne their continents.
The ox hath therefore stretched his yoke in vain,
The ploughman lost his sweat, and the green corn
Hath rotted ere his youth attained a beard.
The fold stands empty in the drownèd field,
And crows are fatted with the murrion flock;
The nine-men's-morris is filled up with mud,
And the quaint mazes in the wanton green
For lack of tread are undistinguishable.
The human mortals want their winter cheer;
No night is now with hymn or carol blessed.
Therefore the moon, the governess of floods,
Pale in her anger, washes all the air,
That rheumatic diseases do abound;
And through this distemperature we see
The seasons alter; hoary-headed frosts
Fall in the fresh lap of the crimson rose,
And on old Hiems' thin and icy crown
An odorous chaplet of sweet summer buds
Is, as in mockery, set. The spring, the summer,
The childing autumn, angry winter change
Their wonted liveries, and the mazèd world
By their increase now knows not which is which.
And this same progeny of evils comes
From our debate, from our dissension.
We are their parents and original.

Oberon asks Titania to give up her 'changeling boy', the subject of the quarrel. She explains why she is going to keep him, and Oberon promises to be revenged.

1 Titania refuses a male command (in pairs)

With a partner, look carefully at Titania's reasons for keeping the boy (lines 123–37). Once again, a male character is trying to dominate a female character. How persuasive do you think Titania's argument is? Together, choose the most compelling line.

▶ Michelle Pfeiffer played Titania in the 1999 movie of *A Midsummer Night's Dream*. Who would you cast if you had the choice?

Themes

Mirroring mortals

Shakespeare seems to be presenting the fairy world as mirroring relationships in the mortal world. Much of the behaviour and language of the fairies is evocative of human arguments.

Identify the thematic and linguistic echoes of the lovers. For example, the conflict between Helena and Demetrius and its consequences in the lives of others is mirrored in the extreme consequences of Oberon and Titania's disagreement. See if you can find other examples. Suggest why you think Shakespeare structured the play in this way.

Stagecraft

Dual roles

Hippolyta and Titania, and Theseus and Oberon, are quite often played by the same two actors. What problems might an actor encounter playing two characters? Decide on one piece of advice you would give someone who is cast to play both Oberon and Theseus. Write it in your Director's Journal.

henchman page

votress member of religious order, worshipper

embarkèd traders traders who had set sail

wanton mischievous, immoral

swimming gait gliding movement

trifles things of little value

Perchance maybe

dance in our round (fairies traditionally dance in a ring)

spare avoid

haunts places frequently visited

chide downright argue

OBERON Do you amend it, then: it lies in you.
Why should Titania cross her Oberon?
I do but beg a little changeling boy
To be my henchman.

TITANIA Set your heart at rest.
The fairy land buys not the child of me.
His mother was a votress of my order,
And in the spicèd Indian air by night
Full often hath she gossiped by my side,
And sat with me on Neptune's yellow sands
Marking th'embarkèd traders on the flood,
When we have laughed to see the sails conceive
And grow big-bellied with the wanton wind;
Which she, with pretty and with swimming gait
Following (her womb then rich with my young squire),
Would imitate, and sail upon the land
To fetch me trifles, and return again
As from a voyage, rich with merchandise.
But she, being mortal, of that boy did die,
And for her sake do I rear up her boy;
And for her sake I will not part with him.

OBERON How long within this wood intend you stay?

TITANIA Perchance till after Theseus' wedding day.
If you will patiently dance in our round,
And see our moonlight revels, go with us:
If not, shun me, and I will spare your haunts.

OBERON Give me that boy, and I will go with thee.

TITANIA Not for thy fairy kingdom! Fairies, away.
We shall chide downright if I longer stay.

Exeunt [*Titania and her train*]

OBERON Well, go thy way. Thou shalt not from this grove
Till I torment thee for this injury.

Oberon tells Puck to fetch him 'love-in-idleness' (a flower touched by Cupid's arrow). When the juice of the flower is put on the eyelids of the sleeping, it makes them fall in love with whatever they first see when they awake.

1 Actions and reactions (in pairs)

The director has asked you to choreograph a pacey and action-packed presentation of Oberon's speech. One of you takes the role of Oberon and the other of Puck. Dramatise Oberon's narrative for the audience. Work out a series of actions for Oberon and reactions for Puck. Present your performance to another pair, or to the class.

Since when

promontory rocks that overlook the sea

dulcet soothing, sweet

rude rough

certain accurate

vestal virgin (possibly an allusion to Queen Elizabeth I)

Cupid's fiery shaft Cupid's arrow, which was supposed to make the person hit fall in love

chaste pure

imperial votress (again, a possible reference to Queen Elizabeth I?)

In maiden meditation thinking her young woman's thoughts (still free of entanglement in love)

bolt arrow

madly dote / Upon fall madly in love with

leviathan whale

girdle (Puck circles Earth like a girdle or belt)

My gentle Puck, come hither. Thou rememberest
Since once I sat upon a promontory,
And heard a mermaid on a dolphin's back
Uttering such dulcet and harmonious breath
That the rude sea grew civil at her song,
And certain stars shot madly from their spheres
To hear the sea-maid's music?

PUCK I remember.

OBERON That very time I saw (but thou couldst not)
Flying between the cold moon and the earth
Cupid all armed: a certain aim he took
At a fair vestal thronèd by the west,
And loosed his loveshaft smartly from his bow
As it should pierce a hundred thousand hearts;
But I might see young Cupid's fiery shaft
Quenched in the chaste beams of the watery moon;
And the imperial votress passèd on
In maiden meditation, fancy-free.
Yet marked I where the bolt of Cupid fell:
It fell upon a little western flower,
Before, milk-white; now purple with love's wound:
And maidens call it 'love-in-idleness'.
Fetch me that flower, the herb I showed thee once;
The juice of it on sleeping eyelids laid
Will make or man or woman madly dote
Upon the next live creature that it sees.
Fetch me this herb, and be thou here again
Ere the leviathan can swim a league.

PUCK I'll put a girdle round about the earth
In forty minutes! [*Exit*]

Oberon plans to use the flower's juice on Titania, then makes himself invisible as Demetrius and Helena enter, arguing. Demetrius is looking for Hermia, and Helena has followed him.

1 Would you rather…

Read lines 180–1 in the script opposite. Would you rather fall in love with a:

- lion
- bear
- wolf
- bull
- monkey
- ape?

What kind of person does each of these animals suggest? Write down your ideas.

2 Oberon's revenge – your view

a Read aloud Oberon's lines 176–85. Write a list of what they reveal about his character. If he were human, is he someone you would like, respect, admire, fear, distrust or something else? What adjective would you use to describe him?

b Write your word on a large sheet of paper. Add a quotation to support your choice, and give some analysis of it. In turn, hold your word up for the class to see and spend a few seconds defending your ideas. Through discussion, come to a class consensus of the best words and quotations.

3 'I am your spaniel' (in pairs)

One person takes the role of Demetrius, the other of Helena. Read lines 188–213 out loud. Discuss what you think of this exchange. (You may want to look at 'Love and marriage', p. 151, and 'Women in Elizabethan England', p. 154.)

Stagecraft

The Fairy King and the audience (in small groups)

a Oberon is on the stage alone at first. His soliloquy tells of his intended revenge. Speculate on the kind of relationship Shakespeare envisaged him having with the audience here. In particular, discuss whether he might speak some or all of his lines directly to the audience.

b 'I am invisible' – easy enough to achieve in a movie, but how could you accomplish this on stage? Discuss this in your group and then write your ideas in your Director's Journal.

render up hand over

conference conversation

wood (line 192) mad, insane, while he is in a real wood (Elizabethans were fond of wordplay and puns)

adamant hard stone, diamond

Leave you give up

your spaniel your subservient dog (a very disturbing image to modern ears)

fawn seek attention and affection by behaving submissively

spurn reject

OBERON Having once this juice
I'll watch Titania when she is asleep,
And drop the liquor of it in her eyes:
The next thing then she, waking, looks upon –
Be it on lion, bear, or wolf, or bull,
On meddling monkey, or on busy ape –
She shall pursue it with the soul of love.
And ere I take this charm from off her sight
(As I can take it with another herb)
I'll make her render up her page to me.
But who comes here? I am invisible,
And I will overhear their conference.

Enter DEMETRIUS, HELENA *following him.*

DEMETRIUS I love thee not, therefore pursue me not.
Where is Lysander, and fair Hermia?
The one I'll slay, the other slayeth me.
Thou told'st me they were stol'n unto this wood,
And here am I, and wood within this wood
Because I cannot meet my Hermia.
Hence, get thee gone, and follow me no more.

HELENA You draw me, you hard-hearted adamant!
But yet you draw not iron, for my heart
Is true as steel. Leave you your power to draw,
And I shall have no power to follow you.

DEMETRIUS Do I entice you? Do I speak you fair?
Or rather do I not in plainest truth
Tell you I do not, nor I cannot love you?

HELENA And even for that do I love you the more.
I am your spaniel; and, Demetrius,
The more you beat me I will fawn on you.
Use me but as your spaniel: spurn me, strike me,
Neglect me, lose me; only give me leave,
Unworthy as I am, to follow you.
What worser place can I beg in your love
(And yet a place of high respect with me)
Than to be usèd as you use your dog?

DEMETRIUS Tempt not too much the hatred of my spirit;
For I am sick when I do look on thee.

HELENA And I am sick when I look not on you.

Helena continues to woo Demetrius. He is angry and frustrated at her persistence, and eventually he runs off. She follows him.

Themes

Power and control

a The physical threat Women often feel more vulnerable at night, especially in isolated places such as a wood. The problem of women's safety at night was as real in Shakespeare's day as it is today. Try speaking Demetrius's lines in a number of ways: menacing, anxious, irritated, frustrated, bored and other ideas of your own. Consider how each reading potentially changes Shakespeare's purpose with this scene.

b The moral threat Shakespeare may not have been considering Helena's physical safety as much as the threat to her reputation and respectability. Either way, this scene adds an unpleasantly hard edge to what is surely a light-hearted play. What other 'hard edges' have you noticed so far in the play?

Characters

Demetrius

Demetrius is a problem character. His language is unpleasant and aggressive in this scene and yet he is a lover, implying that he is a character deserving of the audience's sympathy. How would you play him in Acts 1 and 2? Write down some ideas and consider audience reaction. Also note any parallels between Demetrius, Theseus, Oberon and Egeus.

1 Write a couplet for Demetrius

Helena's final couplet (the two rhyming lines 243–4) sums up her feelings. Write a couplet for Demetrius to say to Helena just before he leaves to sum up his own feelings.

impeach call into question

desert lonely, deserted

brakes undergrowth, thicket

Apollo flies … chase the story (well known in Shakepeare's time) of Daphne, who runs away to avoid the embraces of Apollo; she was changed into a laurel tree as punishment

griffin beast that is half eagle and half lion

hind doe (female deer)

stay endure

do thee mischief harm you

Fie exclamation that shows shock or disgust

upon by means of

DEMETRIUS You do impeach your modesty too much,
To leave the city and commit yourself
Into the hands of one that loves you not;
To trust the opportunity of night,
And the ill counsel of a desert place,
With the rich worth of your virginity.

HELENA Your virtue is my privilege: for that
It is not night when I do see your face,
Therefore I think I am not in the night;
Nor doth this wood lack worlds of company,
For you, in my respect, are all the world.
Then how can it be said I am alone
When all the world is here to look on me?

DEMETRIUS I'll run from thee and hide me in the brakes,
And leave thee to the mercy of wild beasts.

HELENA The wildest hath not such a heart as you.
Run when you will: the story shall be changed;
Apollo flies, and Daphne holds the chase,
The dove pursues the griffin, the mild hind
Makes speed to catch the tiger – bootless speed,
When cowardice pursues, and valour flies!

DEMETRIUS I will not stay thy questions. Let me go;
Or if thou follow me, do not believe
But I shall do thee mischief in the wood.

HELENA Ay, in the temple, in the town, the field,
You do me mischief. Fie, Demetrius,
Your wrongs do set a scandal on my sex!
We cannot fight for love, as men may do;
We should be wooed, and were not made to woo.

[*Exit Demetrius*]

I'll follow thee, and make a heaven of hell,
To die upon the hand I love so well. *Exit*

Oberon vows to help Helena. Puck returns with the flower. Oberon will use it on Titania when she is asleep. He tells Puck to drop the juice of it in Demetrius's eyes when Helena is near.

Themes

Power and control

This scene ends with Oberon's decision to use the magic 'love-in-idleness' flower (line 168) to dominate his wife and fill her mind with 'hateful fantasies.' In Act 1 Scene 1 we see Theseus, after subduing Hippolyta through war and courtship, making a decisive judgement on Hermia's future by siding with her father. Make a list of other ways in which Shakespeare mirrors the mortal world with that of the fairies.

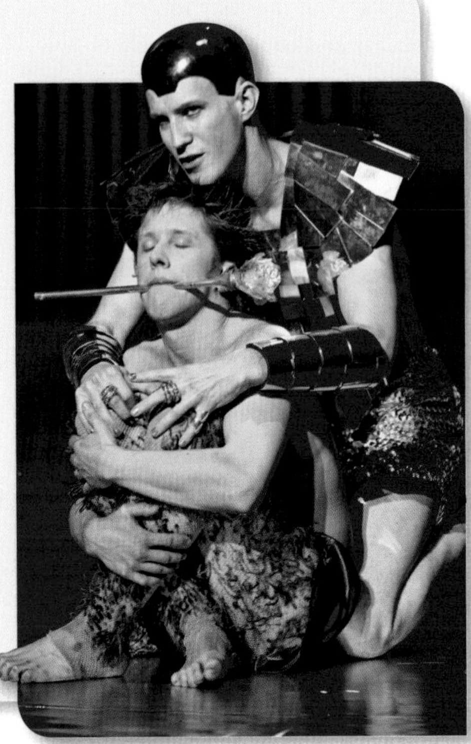

nymph beautiful woodland creature

grove wood

oxlip flowering herb, hybrid of cowslip and primrose

overcanopied covered over with shade

woodbine honeysuckle

sometime of during

enamelled metal-like, bright, shiny

Weed cloth

espies sees

Stagecraft

Out of this world

Costume designers, hair stylists and make-up artists can have a lot of fun developing ideas for presenting the fairies. Choose Oberon, Titania or Puck and design a concept for their costume, hair and make-up. Either draw it or describe it in your Director's Journal.

OBERON Fare thee well, nymph. Ere he do leave this grove
Thou shalt fly him, and he shall seek thy love.

Enter Puck.

Hast thou the flower there? Welcome, wanderer.
PUCK Ay, there it is.
OBERON I pray thee give it me.
I know a bank where the wild thyme blows,
Where oxlips and the nodding violet grows,
Quite overcanopied with luscious woodbine,
With sweet musk-roses, and with eglantine:
There sleeps Titania sometime of the night,
Lulled in these flowers with dances and delight;
And there the snake throws her enamelled skin,
Weed wide enough to wrap a fairy in;
And with the juice of this I'll streak her eyes,
And make her full of hateful fantasies.
Take thou some of it, and seek through this grove:
A sweet Athenian lady is in love
With a disdainful youth; anoint his eyes,
But do it when the next thing he espies
May be the lady. Thou shalt know the man
By the Athenian garments he hath on.
Effect it with some care, that he may prove
More fond on her than she upon her love.
And look thou meet me ere the first cock crow.
PUCK Fear not, my lord; your servant shall do so.

Exeunt

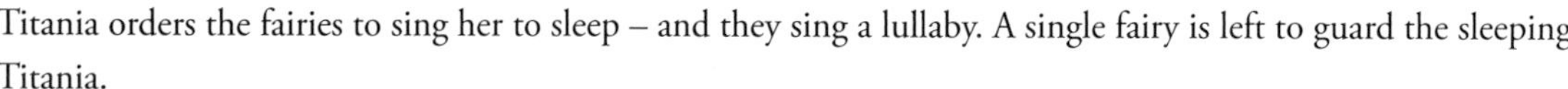

Titania orders the fairies to sing her to sleep – and they sing a lullaby. A single fairy is left to guard the sleeping Titania.

Characters

+ - ? (plus, minus, puzzling)

With Titania, Shakespeare has drawn an interesting and complex character (see 'Titania', p. 157). Make notes on what you think of Titania so far, in three columns – positive, negative and puzzling.

+ What do you like about her?
- What do you dislike?
? What do you find puzzling?

Begin a file on Titania where you note her most interesting words and phrases, analyse them and comment on what they reveal of her character. Add to your notes each time Titania appears in a scene.

Language in the play

Fairy language

The fairies here sing a lullaby for Titania to send her to sleep. Decide your two favourite lines and explore what in particular you like about them. Think about how the fairies' language and imagery paint a picture of the fairy world. Using your quotations and analysis as a starting point, write a paragraph addressing the following question: 'How do Shakespeare's language choices help us understand the fairy world?'

roundel dance in a circle

cankers caterpillars
reremice bats
leathern leathery

quaint dainty
offices jobs

double tongue forked tongue

Philomel nightingale

Hence go away

offence harm

aloof at a distance
sentinel lookout/guard

Act 2 Scene 2
The wood

Enter TITANIA, *Queen of Fairies, with her train.*

TITANIA Come, now a roundel and a fairy song,
Then for the third part of a minute, hence –
Some to kill cankers in the musk-rose buds,
Some war with reremice for their leathern wings
To make my small elves coats, and some keep back
The clamorous owl that nightly hoots and wonders
At our quaint spirits. Sing me now asleep;
Then to your offices, and let me rest.

Fairies sing.

[FIRST FAIRY] You spotted snakes with double tongue,
Thorny hedgehogs, be not seen.
Newts and blindworms, do no wrong,
Come not near our Fairy Queen.

[CHORUS] Philomel with melody
Sing in our sweet lullaby,
Lulla, lulla, lullaby; lulla, lulla, lullaby.
Never harm
Nor spell nor charm
Come our lovely lady nigh.
So good night, with lullaby.

FIRST FAIRY Weaving spiders, come not here;
Hence, you longlegged spinners, hence!
Beetles black approach not near;
Worm nor snail, do no offence.

[CHORUS] Philomel with melody
Sing in our sweet lullaby,
Lulla, lulla, lullaby; lulla, lulla, lullaby.
Never harm
Nor spell nor charm
Come our lovely lady nigh.
So good night, with lullaby.

Titania sleeps.

SECOND FAIRY Hence, away! Now all is well;
One aloof stand sentinel!

[*Exeunt Fairies*]

Oberon puts the flower's juice on Titania's eyes with a charm that she will wake 'when some vile thing is near!' and fall in love with it. Lysander and Hermia enter, lost. She rejects his advances and they prepare to sleep.

Language in the play

Oberon's spell

Shakespeare fills Oberon's spell (lines 33–40) with animal symbolism. Write a list of the animals that are included and suggest what each might represent. What effect does this have on Oberon's spell? Do you think his final line, 'Wake when some vile thing is near!' is intended to be sinister, amusing, vengeful, evil or something else? Summarise your conclusion in one sentence.

1 Would you rather…

Read through lines 32–40 again. Would you rather be transformed into a:

- cat
- bear
- leopard
- boar?

Explain your choice to the class.

Characters

Lysander and Hermia (in pairs)

Shakespeare includes an intimate scene between Lysander and Hermia here, and the audience learns a great deal about them and their relationship. With a partner, choose which lines are the most important in helping us understand the nature of their feelings for each other. Then carry out the following tasks:

a One of you focuses on Hermia's perspective and the other on Lysander's. Write for five minutes describing their feelings as they lie falling asleep under the trees. What are they thinking about: what has happened so far, the difference of opinion they have just had, or their plans and hopes for the future? Use first-person narrative and try to write in **rhyming couplets** (two lines of the same length that rhyme), as Shakespeare does here, if you want a challenge.

b Read your responses aloud to each other. Decide if this scene has changed your impressions of these characters. Who do you most empathise with, and why? Report your main ideas back to the class.

languish droop, pine

ounce lynx

Pard leopard

troth truth

in love's conference in the conversation of lovers

knit united

much beshrew a curse upon

Enter OBERON; [*he squeezes the juice on Titania's eyes*].

OBERON
What thou seest when thou dost wake,
Do it for thy true love take;
Love and languish for his sake.
Be it ounce or cat or bear,
Pard, or boar with bristled hair
In thy eye that shall appear
When thou wak'st, it is thy dear.
Wake when some vile thing is near! [*Exit*]

Enter LYSANDER *and* HERMIA.

LYSANDER
Fair love, you faint with wandering in the wood,
And, to speak truth, I have forgot our way.
We'll rest us, Hermia, if you think it good,
And tarry for the comfort of the day.

HERMIA
Be it so, Lysander; find you out a bed,
For I upon this bank will rest my head.

LYSANDER
One turf shall serve as pillow for us both;
One heart, one bed, two bosoms, and one troth.

HERMIA
Nay, good Lysander, for my sake, my dear,
Lie further off yet; do not lie so near.

LYSANDER
O take the sense, sweet, of my innocence!
Love takes the meaning in love's conference;
I mean that my heart unto yours is knit,
So that but one heart we can make of it:
Two bosoms interchainèd with an oath,
So then two bosoms and a single troth.
Then by your side no bed-room me deny,
For lying so, Hermia, I do not lie.

HERMIA
Lysander riddles very prettily.
Now much beshrew my manners and my pride
If Hermia meant to say Lysander lied.
But, gentle friend, for love and courtesy
Lie further off, in human modesty;
Such separation as may well be said
Becomes a virtuous bachelor and a maid,
So far be distant, and good night, sweet friend;
Thy love ne'er alter till thy sweet life end!

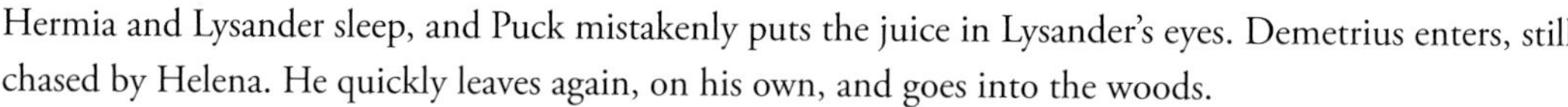

Hermia and Lysander sleep, and Puck mistakenly puts the juice in Lysander's eyes. Demetrius enters, still chased by Helena. He quickly leaves again, on his own, and goes into the woods.

Stagecraft

The fairy touch (in pairs)

In this scene, the fairy world – through Puck – directly manipulates the feelings of a mortal. Every new production of the play spends time in rehearsal working out how to present the interactions and the impact they have, because the consequences of such influence could be disturbing, catastrophic or amusing.

How would you want Puck to speak and behave here? In your pair, decide how you think Puck's speech and transformation of Lysander should be performed. Take roles, one person as Puck and the other as director. Act out Puck's speech, focusing on his attitude to the mortal whose life he is changing. Swap roles and direct Puck to display different attitudes – try mischievous, sinister, comic and other ideas of your own. Add notes to your Director's Journal.

▲ *Hermia and Lysander*, by John Simmons (1870).

Language in the play

Rhyme versus syntax

There are over 700 rhyming lines in *A Midsummer Night's Dream*. Actors always talk together about whether the rhymes should be emphasised. Some argue they should; others claim that the syntax (word order) is more important, so that the meaning is clearly conveyed to the audience. They say that the lines should 'run on' where appropriate, to bring out the meaning.

Try out the two approaches using Puck's speech in lines 72–89.

approve put to the proof

Weeds clothes

dank damp

durst not dares not

lack-love someone who avoids love

kill-courtesy someone with no manners or respect

Churl heartless rogue

owe possess

darkling sad or dark one

LYSANDER Amen, amen, to that fair prayer say I,
And then end life when I end loyalty!
Here is my bed; sleep give thee all his rest.
HERMIA With half that wish the wisher's eyes be pressed.
They sleep.

Enter PUCK.

PUCK Through the forest have I gone,
But Athenian found I none
On whose eyes I might approve
This flower's force in stirring love.
Night and silence – Who is here?
Weeds of Athens he doth wear:
This is he my master said
Despisèd the Athenian maid;
And here the maiden, sleeping sound
On the dank and dirty ground.
Pretty soul, she durst not lie
Near this lack-love, this kill-courtesy.
Churl, upon thy eyes I throw
All the power this charm doth owe.
[*He squeezes the juice on Lysander's eyes.*]
When thou wak'st let love forbid
Sleep his seat on thy eyelid.
So, awake when I am gone;
For I must now to Oberon. *Exit*

Enter DEMETRIUS *and* HELENA, *running.*

HELENA Stay, though thou kill me, sweet Demetrius!
DEMETRIUS I charge thee, hence, and do not haunt me thus.
HELENA O wilt thou darkling leave me? Do not so!
DEMETRIUS Stay, on thy peril; I alone will go. *Exit*

Helena stops to rest and sees Lysander. He wakes up, and immediately falls in love with Helena because of the flower's magic.

Characters

Helena

a Which phrase or line in Helena's speech in the script opposite is the most revealing of her character? Choose one, and write two or three comments on what it suggests about her.

b Now look back at Helena's speeches in Act 1 and consider how she has developed as a character. The audience has always seen Helena in relation to her suffering at Demetrius's rejection. In what ways has this been developed by Shakespeare in Act 2? Write a paragraph in which you explain your ideas about Helena and integrate quotations to support them.

1 Lysander – 'raw passion'? (in pairs)

An actor who played Lysander said: 'Lysander gets taken over when he's under the influence of magic; that's where character tends to disappear. It brings out all this raw passion.' Discuss with a partner what the actor means by this. What directions would you give to someone playing the part of Lysander here?

2 The dance of the lovers – who loves whom? (II)

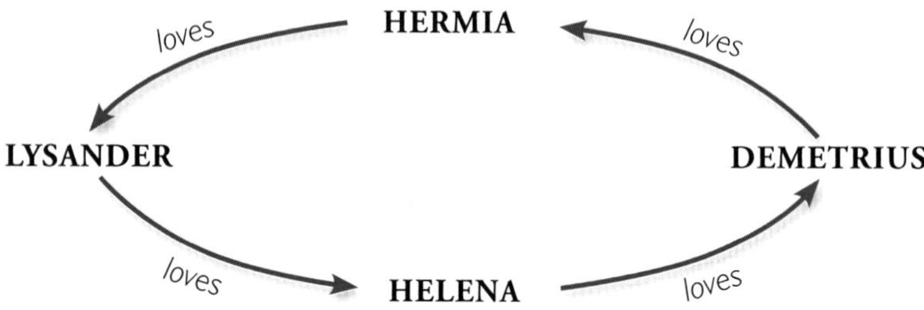

Look back at the diagram on page 10, and discuss the changed relationships shown here.

fond foolish

The more … my grace the more I pray, the less I get in return

dissembling concealing, disguising

glass mirror

sphery eyne star-like eyes

Transparent honest, open

ripe mature

touching reaching

Reason … to my will reason or rationality can be arranged by the force of my will

o'erlook read through

HELENA O, I am out of breath in this fond chase!
The more my prayer, the lesser is my grace.
Happy is Hermia, wheresoe'er she lies,
For she hath blessèd and attractive eyes.
How came her eyes so bright? Not with salt tears –
If so, my eyes are oftener washed than hers.
No, no, I am as ugly as a bear,
For beasts that meet me run away for fear.
Therefore no marvel though Demetrius
Do as a monster fly my presence thus.
What wicked and dissembling glass of mine
Made me compare with Hermia's sphery eyne?
But who is here? – Lysander, on the ground?
Dead, or asleep? I see no blood, no wound.
Lysander, if you live, good sir, awake!

LYSANDER [*Waking*.]
And run through fire I will for thy sweet sake!
Transparent Helena, nature shows art
That through thy bosom makes me see thy heart.
Where is Demetrius? O, how fit a word
Is that vile name to perish on my sword!

HELENA Do not say so, Lysander, say not so.
What though he love your Hermia? Lord, what though?
Yet Hermia still loves you; then be content.

LYSANDER Content with Hermia? No; I do repent
The tedious minutes I with her have spent.
Not Hermia, but Helena I love.
Who will not change a raven for a dove?
The will of man is by his reason swayed,
And reason says you are the worthier maid.
Things growing are not ripe until their season;
So I, being young, till now ripe not to reason.
And touching now the point of human skill,
Reason becomes the marshal to my will.
And leads me to your eyes, where I o'erlook
Love's stories written in love's richest book.

Helena thinks Lysander is making fun of her, and leaves. He follows, leaving Hermia behind, still asleep. Hermia wakes from a nightmare, realises she is alone and goes to find Lysander.

1 Three moods, three 'dreams' (in threes)

There are three characters, three moods and three different 'dreams' here. None of the three characters really understands what is going on.

a Each person chooses a character, reads their speech aloud and describes the character's mood – their 'dream' of what is happening.

b Now all concentrate on Hermia's dream. Discuss what it might mean. Share views on whether you agree that dreams sometimes highlight subconscious fears or obsessions. Give examples if you can.

c Together, compare the women's speeches in the script opposite and see if there are any similarities. Then contrast them with Lysander's. If you find differences between the male and female speeches, share them with another group and discuss the implications.

Language in the play

Disturbing images

Remind yourselves of the 'dance' of the lovers on page 50 – things couldn't get any worse. List as many negative/upsetting images as you can find in lines 94–162. When you have compiled your list, write a few sentences about how the images suggest that the midsummer night's dream is becoming a nightmare.

Themes

Dreams and reality (in pairs)

Which is worse – Hermia's dream or her reality? Individually, write your response, justifying your ideas. Then read your partner's work, and underline what you consider to be the best sentence in their response. Read this sentence aloud to the class and explain what you like about it.

keen sharp

flout mock
insufficiency inabillity
Good troth truly
good sooth in truth, indeed
perforce of necessity

surfeit surplus

heresies false religious beliefs

of all loves for love's sake
swoon faint
nigh near

HELENA Wherefore was I to this keen mockery born?
When at your hands did I deserve this scorn?
Is't not enough, is't not enough, young man,
That I did never, no, nor never can
Deserve a sweet look from Demetrius' eye
But you must flout my insufficiency?
Good troth, you do me wrong, good sooth, you do,
In such disdainful manner me to woo!
But fare you well: perforce I must confess
I thought you lord of more true gentleness.
O, that a lady of one man refused
Should of another therefore be abused! *Exit*

LYSANDER She sees not Hermia. Hermia, sleep thou there,
And never mayst thou come Lysander near.
For, as a surfeit of the sweetest things
The deepest loathing to the stomach brings,
Or as the heresies that men do leave
Are hated most of those they did deceive,
So thou, my surfeit and my heresy,
Of all be hated, but the most of me!
And, all my powers, address your love and might
To honour Helen, and to be her knight. *Exit*

HERMIA [*Waking.*]
Help me, Lysander, help me! Do thy best
To pluck this crawling serpent from my breast!
Ay me, for pity! What a dream was here!
Lysander, look how I do quake with fear –
Methought a serpent ate my heart away,
And you sat smiling at his cruel prey.
Lysander! What, removed? Lysander, lord!
What, out of hearing? Gone? No sound, no word?
Alack, where are you? Speak and if you hear.
Speak, of all loves! I swoon almost with fear.
No? Then I well perceive you are not nigh.
Either death or you I'll find immediately. *Exit*

Looking back at Act 2
Activities for groups or individuals

1 Male dominance

In his speeches, Oberon shows his power over the lives of both mortals and fairies. This reinforces the sense that male characters dominate the play (Theseus in Athens, Oberon in the wood). In the production shown on this page, Oberon's power over his surroundings was reflected in dramatic staging and special effects. Perhaps Shakespeare is replicating the realities of his time, or perhaps this reflects the characters' positions of status and power: duke and king.

Discuss whether by depicting the male characters Egeus, Theseus and Demetrius as oppressive and cruel, Shakespeare is encouraging the audience to side with the women.

2 Love and magic: ancient and modern

In Scene 1, lines 155–74, Oberon tells of the flower whose juice on a sleeper's eyelids makes them 'madly dote' on the first person they see when they wake. The idea of love potions is ancient, but even today a connection is often made between love and magic. Songwriters continue to play with this connection.

Find one modern song that uses the language of love and magic, and bring in the lyrics to share with the class.

3 Characters from myth and legend

Indeed your grandams' maids set a bowl of milk out for Robin Goodfellow . . . the mare, the man in the oak, the puckle, hobgoblin.

This quotation comes from a book Shakespeare probably read, called *The Discovery of Witchcraft*, which was written in 1584. The book describes incidents similar to those the Fairy and Puck talk about at the beginning of Act 2, but, as the quotation implies, hardly anyone believed in Puck (or Robin Goodfellow, as he was often known) any more. Think about what effect is created by using these imaginary characters from myth and superstition in this particular play.

Look carefully at the print of Robin Goodfellow above, which was made in 1639. Describe in detail what you see. Here, Robin appears demonic, with his cloven hooves and horns, surrounded by witches. The image suggests that he is more sexually sinister than the character of Puck in *A Midsummer Night's Dream*. What do you think? Consider the character of Puck in the play in light of this contextual information, and be prepared to contribute to a class discussion. (See also 'Fairies and magic', pp. 153–4 for more on Robin Goodfellow). Keep all this in mind as you watch Puck's role develop further in Act 3.

In the wood near the sleeping Titania, the Mechanicals begin their rehearsal. Bottom suggests changes in the play to make it less frightening.

Stagecraft

'Enter the Clowns'

Shakespeare describes the Mechanicals as 'Clowns' in the stage directions. How might this affect the way a director decides to portray them on stage? What effect do you think Shakespeare hoped this would have on the audience?

a Imagine that you are the director. What would be your first thoughts on reading this stage direction? Make a few notes on this in your Director's Journal.

b The stage directions for this scene also specify that 'TITANIA *remains on stage, asleep*'. Again from the director's perspective, comment on where you would position Titania on stage. Sketch a plan. Remember that the audience needs to be aware she is there, but she must not get in the way of the action.

1 Who is who? (in pairs)

With a partner, decide who is who in the photograph above, and label the characters. Choose a quotation from the script opposite as an appropriate caption for this photograph of the Mechanicals.

Are we all met? are we all here?

Pat on the dot, on time

tiring-house dressing room

bully (adjective that implies respect and admiration)

By'r lakin by Our Lady (an exclamation)

parlous dangerous, terrible

Not a whit not at all

prologue introduction, background information

eight and six rhyme of a ballad (line of eight syllables followed by line of six syllables)

wildfowl half lion, half bird

defect (Bottom probably means 'effect' here)

Act 3 Scene 1
The wood

Enter the Clowns [,BOTTOM, QUINCE, SNOUT, STARVELING, SNUG *and* FLUTE. TITANIA *remains on stage, asleep*].

BOTTOM Are we all met?

QUINCE Pat, pat; and here's a marvellous convenient place for our rehearsal. This green plot shall be our stage, this hawthorn brake our tiring-house, and we will do it in action as we will do it before the Duke.

BOTTOM Peter Quince!

QUINCE What sayest thou, bully Bottom?

BOTTOM There are things in this comedy of Pyramus and Thisbe that will never please. First, Pyramus must draw a sword to kill himself, which the ladies cannot abide. How answer you that?

SNOUT By'r lakin, a parlous fear!

STARVELING I believe we must leave the killing out, when all is done.

BOTTOM Not a whit; I have a device to make all well. Write me a prologue, and let the prologue seem to say we will do no harm with our swords, and that Pyramus is not killed indeed; and for the more better assurance, tell them that I, Pyramus, am not Pyramus, but Bottom the weaver: this will put them out of fear.

QUINCE Well, we will have such a prologue; and it shall be written in eight and six.

BOTTOM No, make it two more: let it be written in eight and eight.

SNOUT Will not the ladies be afeard of the lion?

STARVELING I fear it, I promise you.

BOTTOM Masters, you ought to consider with yourself, to bring in (God shield us!) a lion among ladies is a most dreadful thing; for there is not a more fearful wildfowl than your lion living; and we ought to look to't.

SNOUT Therefore another prologue must tell he is not a lion.

BOTTOM Nay, you must name his name, and half his face must be seen through the lion's neck, and he himself must speak through, saying thus, or to the same defect: 'Ladies', or 'Fair ladies, I would wish you', or 'I would request you', or 'I would entreat you, not to fear, not to tremble: my life for yours. If you think I come hither as a lion, it were pity of my life. No, I am no such thing; I am a man,

The Mechanicals discuss how to show moonlight and the wall in the play, and decide they must have an actor represent each.

1 Act it out! (in sevens)

The first half of this scene shows the Mechanicals preparing to rehearse, and Puck's mischievous interference. To gain a first impression of what happens, take parts as the Mechanicals and Puck and read lines 1–98. Don't pause over anything you don't understand – just enjoy the comedy. When you have completed your read-through, the group should split into two and work on some of the activities below.

2 Bottom and the play (in groups of three or four)

In your group, allocate one task to each person from the following list (each task should be written up in around 300 words):

a Pick up as many clues as you can in this scene about the play that Quince has written. Outline the characters and the storyline of the play the Mechanicals propose to perform.

b Complete a character study of Bottom, with quotations.

c Research the original story of Pyramus and Thisbe, two ill-fated lovers, and summarise it.

d Read lines 1–59 of this scene from a director's perspective, and write detailed directions for each character. Record your ideas in your Director's Journal.

Read each others' work and then discuss what you have learnt about Shakespeare's choices in this scene.

▶ What do you think Bottom is saying here?

almanac calendar that often includes astronomical information

casement hinged window

disfigure change appearance (Quince has used the wrong word here – he means 'figure', as in 'represent')

chink gap

loam clay for brick-making

rough-cast rough coating for a wall

as other men are' – and there indeed let him name his name, and tell them plainly he is Snug the joiner.

QUINCE Well, it shall be so. But there is two hard things: that is, to bring the moonlight into a chamber; for, you know, Pyramus and Thisbe meet by moonlight.

SNUG Doth the moon shine that night we play our play?

BOTTOM A calendar, a calendar! Look in the almanac – find out moonshine, find out moonshine!

QUINCE Yes, it doth shine that night.

BOTTOM Why, then may you leave a casement of the great chamber window, where we play, open, and the moon may shine in at the casement.

QUINCE Ay; or else one must come in with a bush of thorns and a lantern, and say he comes to disfigure, or to present the person of Moonshine. Then there is another thing: we must have a wall in the great chamber; for Pyramus and Thisbe, says the story, did talk through the chink of a wall.

SNOUT You can never bring in a wall. What say you, Bottom?

BOTTOM Some man or other must present Wall; and let him have some plaster, or some loam, or some rough-cast about him to signify Wall; or let him hold his fingers thus, and through that cranny shall Pyramus and Thisbe whisper.

QUINCE If that may be, then all is well. Come, sit down every mother's son, and rehearse your parts. Pyramus, you begin. When you have spoken your speech, enter into the brake, and so everyone according to his cue.

Puck enters, and watches as the Mechanicals begin to rehearse, going off with Bottom when he goes off stage. After getting his lines muddled, Flute gives Bottom his cue to reappear.

Characters

'*Enter* PUCK' (in pairs)

The audience is watching Puck, who is watching the Mechanicals' rehearsal. He asks, 'What hempen homespuns have we swaggering here ..?' How does this line help us visualise the characters? Clearly, Puck is amused. But is his amusement born of ridicule, affection or contempt? With a partner, decide how he should say the line.

▲'What hempen homespuns have we swaggering here … ?'

1 A rehearsal – and bad acting (in threes)

Not only is there a play within a play in *A Midsummer Night's Dream* (in Act 5), there are even rehearsals. Many people think that Shakespeare was mocking groups of actors who travelled around England in the early years of Queen Elizabeth I's reign. Others think he was poking fun at amateur dramatics because he was in one of the first professional theatre companies in England. Whatever the reason, Shakespeare knew how to present bad acting.

First, talk together about the complications of playing characters who are attempting to act well, but failing. Then take parts as Quince, Bottom and Flute, and speak lines 65–84 to show how the timing of the lines helps to reveal the Mechanicals' lack of acting ability.

hempen homespuns the Mechanicals are dressed in rough, homemade clothes

swaggering showing off

cradle bed

toward in preparation

odious savours sweet sweet hateful perfumes

[odorous] savours sweet sweet-smelling perfumes; Bottom mistakes 'odorous' (smelling) for 'odours' (smells), which makes the phrase meaningless

by and by in a moment

lilywhite of hue pale in colour

triumphant magnificent

brisky juvenal lively young man

eke also

Jew this could be Flute's misreading of 'jewel'

Ninny's fool's (Flute mistakes 'Ninny' for 'Ninus', an ancient king)

cue prompt to start speaking your lines (in Shakespeare's theatre, actors were not given the whole script – just their own lines and the cues to begin speaking)

Enter PUCK.

PUCK What hempen homespuns have we swaggering here
So near the cradle of the Fairy Queen?
What, a play toward? I'll be an auditor,
An actor too perhaps, if I see cause.

QUINCE Speak, Pyramus! Thisbe, stand forth!

BOTTOM (*as Pyramus*)
Thisbe, the flowers of odious savours sweet –

QUINCE Odours – 'odorous'!

BOTTOM (*as Pyramus*) . . . odours savours sweet.
So hath thy breath, my dearest Thisbe dear.
But hark, a voice! Stay thou but here awhile,
And by and by I will to thee appear. *Exit*

PUCK A stranger Pyramus than e'er played here. [*Exit*]

FLUTE Must I speak now?

QUINCE Ay, marry must you; for you must understand he goes but to see a noise that he heard, and is to come again.

FLUTE (*as Thisbe*)
Most radiant Pyramus, most lilywhite of hue,
Of colour like the red rose on triumphant briar,
Most brisky juvenal, and eke most lovely Jew,
As true as truest horse that yet would never tire,
I'll meet thee, Pyramus, at Ninny's tomb –

QUINCE 'Ninus' tomb', man! – Why, you must not speak that yet; that you answer to Pyramus. You speak all your part at once, cues and all. Pyramus, enter – your cue is past. It is 'never tire'.

FLUTE O –
(*as Thisbe*)
As true as truest horse, that yet would never tire.

Bottom re-enters with an ass's head (because of Puck's magic), and all his comrades run away. Bottom thinks that they are teasing him to make him frightened. He sings to show he is unafraid.

Stagecraft

'Bottom with the ass head' (in pairs)

a There are only a few moments before Bottom reappears '*with the ass head*'. Suggest ways that this might be accomplished by the make-up and costume designers. What effect would they want to achieve with the audience here?

b List the techniques that Shakespeare uses to highlight the comedy in the script opposite, and explain why this scene is also sad.

round dance

knavery trickery

translated changed, transformed

ousel blackbird
cock male bird
throstle song thrush
little quill quiet song

Enter [Puck], and Bottom with the ass head [on].

BOTTOM (*as Pyramus*)
If I were fair, fair Thisbe, I were only thine.

QUINCE O monstrous! O strange! We are haunted! Pray, masters, fly, masters! Help!

Exeunt Quince, Snug, Flute, Snout and Starveling

PUCK
I'll follow you: I'll lead you about a round,
Through bog, through bush, through brake, through briar;
Sometime a horse I'll be, sometime a hound,
A hog, a headless bear, sometime a fire,
And neigh, and bark, and grunt, and roar, and burn,
Like horse, hound, hog, bear, fire at every turn. *Exit*

BOTTOM Why do they run away? This is a knavery of them to make me afeard.

Enter Snout.

SNOUT O Bottom, thou art changed. What do I see on thee?

BOTTOM What do you see? You see an ass head of your own, do you?

[*Exit Snout*]

Enter Quince.

QUINCE Bless thee, Bottom, bless thee! Thou art translated! *Exit*

BOTTOM I see their knavery. This is to make an ass of me, to fright me, if they could; but I will not stir from this place, do what they can. I will walk up and down here, and will sing, that they shall hear I am not afraid.

[*Sings.*] The ousel cock so black of hue,
With orange-tawny bill,
The throstle with his note so true,
The wren with little quill –

Bottom's song wakes Titania who, under the influence of the potion, instantly falls in love with him. She vows to keep him with her.

Themes

'reason and love keep little company'

The relationship between reason and love is one of the themes of the play, and Bottom's lines 120–1 stress how far they are apart. *A Midsummer Night's Dream* shows vividly how love makes people act very irrationally. Make a list of the characters who you think are being reasonable, and another list of those who are dominated by their emotions, particularly love.

'What angel wakes me from my flowery bed?' This is one of Shakespeare's most famous lines. It is ironic. Why?

1 Bottom – 'wise' and 'beautiful'? (in small groups)

Titania is clearly talking nonsense about Bottom. On the one hand this creates comedy and is amusing for the audience, but do you think Shakespeare might also be making a point about the way people behave when they are in love? If so, what is this point? Discuss with your group and present your thoughts to the class as a whole.

plainsong simple melody

set his wit to set his wits against, argue with

give … lie contradict, call a liar

enthrallèd captivated

gleek joke

of no common rate not ordinary

still doth tend always attends

purge … grossness remove human coarseness

airy spirit fairy creature

TITANIA [*Waking*.] What angel wakes me from my flowery bed?

BOTTOM [*Sings*.]

The finch, the sparrow, and the lark,
The plainsong cuckoo grey,
Whose note full many a man doth mark
And dares not answer nay –

for indeed, who would set his wit to so foolish a bird? Who would give a bird the lie, though he cry 'cuckoo' never so?

TITANIA I pray thee, gentle mortal, sing again;
Mine ear is much enamoured of thy note.
So is mine eye enthrallèd to thy shape,
And thy fair virtue's force perforce doth move me
On the first view to say, to swear, I love thee.

BOTTOM Methinks, mistress, you should have little reason for that. And yet, to say the truth, reason and love keep little company together nowadays; the more the pity that some honest neighbours will not make them friends. Nay, I can gleek upon occasion.

TITANIA Thou art as wise as thou art beautiful.

BOTTOM Not so neither; but if I had wit enough to get out of this wood, I have enough to serve mine own turn.

TITANIA Out of this wood do not desire to go:
Thou shalt remain here, whether thou wilt or no.
I am a spirit of no common rate;
The summer still doth tend upon my state,
And I do love thee. Therefore go with me.
I'll give thee fairies to attend on thee,
And they shall fetch thee jewels from the deep,
And sing, while thou on pressèd flowers dost sleep;
And I will purge thy mortal grossness so
That thou shalt like an airy spirit go.
Peaseblossom, Cobweb, Moth, and Mustardseed!

Enter four Fairies.

PEASEBLOSSOM Ready.

COBWEB And I.

MOTH And I.

MUSTARDSEED And I.

Titania asks her fairies to look after Bottom. He learns their names. Bottom is then led to Titania's bower.

Language in the play

Titania's love

Look carefully at Titania's speech (lines 174–8). What does the language and imagery reveal about the nature of her love for Bottom? What could be happening on stage as she speaks these lines? Write down your ideas in the form of notes, stage directions or extended commentary.

Characters

Bottom (in small groups)

Bottom is the only character from the mortal world to see and talk to the fairies. Bottom and Titania have both been transformed.

a Discuss what sort of relationship these two characters have. Use the photograph above as part of your discussions.

b Which lines in the script opposite reveal most about each character? Choose one line for Titania and one for Bottom, and think about what each shows about the character. Explain your findings to the rest of the group. Compare your choices.

apricocks apricots

dewberries blackberries

do him courtesies show him politeness

cry … mercy beg your pardon

desire you of ask for

if I cut my finger (cobwebs were used to stop bleeding)

Squash unripe peapod

Peascod peapod

eyes water (strong mustard can make the eyes water)

enforcèd violated, spoiled

ALL Where shall we go?

TITANIA Be kind and courteous to this gentleman:
Hop in his walks and gambol in his eyes;
Feed him with apricocks and dewberries,
With purple grapes, green figs, and mulberries;
The honey-bags steal from the humble-bees,
And for night-tapers crop their waxen thighs,
And light them at the fiery glow-worms' eyes
To have my love to bed, and to arise;
And pluck the wings from painted butterflies
To fan the moonbeams from his sleeping eyes.
Nod to him, elves, and do him courtesies.

PEASEBLOSSOM Hail, mortal!

COBWEB Hail!

MOTH Hail!

MUSTARDSEED Hail!

BOTTOM I cry your worships mercy, heartily. I beseech your worship's name.

COBWEB Cobweb.

BOTTOM I shall desire you of more acquaintance, good Master Cobweb; if I cut my finger I shall make bold with you. Your name, honest gentleman?

PEASEBLOSSOM Peaseblossom.

BOTTOM I pray you commend me to Mistress Squash, your mother, and to Master Peascod, your father. Good Master Peaseblossom, I shall desire you of more acquaintance, too. – Your name, I beseech you, sir?

MUSTARDSEED Mustardseed.

BOTTOM Good Master Mustardseed, I know your patience well. That same cowardly, giant-like ox-beef hath devoured many a gentleman of your house. I promise you, your kindred hath made my eyes water ere now. I desire you of more acquaintance, good Master Mustardseed.

TITANIA Come, wait upon him. Lead him to my bower.
The moon methinks looks with a watery eye,
And when she weeps, weeps every little flower,
Lamenting some enforcèd chastity.
Tie up my lover's tongue; bring him silently.

Exeunt

Oberon wonders who or what Titania now loves. Puck says she loves a 'monster' and explains what he has done to Bottom and the other Mechanicals.

1 Speak it – act it! (in small groups)

Puck tells how he took a hand in the Mechanicals' rehearsal, with hilarious results. Lines 6–34 invite acting out. As one person slowly speaks the lines, the others in the group enact them.

◀ What kind of statement is being made about Oberon and Puck in this production? Look carefully at the use of colours, the styling and the body language. Share your ideas with a partner.

Stagecraft

Retelling the tale

In this scene, Shakespeare chooses to retell the story of Bottom's transformation and Titania's waking in detail. The audience has just seen this on stage. Consider why Shakespeare decides to pause here for this extended narration. What effect does it have on the audience? Note down some suggestions in your Director's Journal.

patches clowns

rude rough

barren sort stupid group of men

nole head

mimic actor

fowler bird-hunter

russet-pated choughs grey-headed jackdaws (crow-like birds)

gun's report gun shot

Sever themselves scatter

apparel clothes

yielders those running away in fear

Act 3 Scene 2
The wood

Enter OBERON, *King of Fairies.*

OBERON I wonder if Titania be awaked;
Then what it was that next came in her eye,
Which she must dote on, in extremity.

Enter PUCK.

Here comes my messenger. How now, mad spirit?
What night-rule now about this haunted grove?

PUCK My mistress with a monster is in love.
Near to her close and consecrated bower,
While she was in her dull and sleeping hour,
A crew of patches, rude mechanicals,
That work for bread upon Athenian stalls,
Were met together to rehearse a play
Intended for great Theseus' nuptial day.
The shallowest thick-skin of that barren sort,
Who Pyramus presented, in their sport
Forsook his scene and entered in a brake,
When I did him at this advantage take:
An ass's nole I fixèd on his head.
Anon his Thisbe must be answerèd,
And forth my mimic comes. When they him spy –
As wild geese that the creeping fowler eye,
Or russet-pated choughs, many in sort,
Rising and cawing at the gun's report,
Sever themselves and madly sweep the sky –
So at his sight away his fellows fly,
And at our stamp here o'er and o'er one falls;
He 'Murder!' cries, and help from Athens calls.
Their sense thus weak, lost with their fears thus strong,
Made senseless things begin to do them wrong,
For briars and thorns at their apparel snatch,
Some sleeves, some hats; from yielders all things catch.

Oberon is pleased to hear that Titania has fallen in love with Bottom. Puck says he has also dealt with the 'Athenian'. Demetrius finds Hermia and tries to court her. She accuses him of having murdered Lysander.

Write about it

Darkness and confusion

Shakespeare uses language to create emotional atmosphere.

a Identify words and images in lines 43–81 that best bring out Hermia's and Demetrius's feelings. Group them in any way that appeals to you or is helpful. For example, you could consider language that is violent. Choose the three or four most interesting words, phrases or images.

b Write for ten minutes in response to the title: 'Explain how Shakespeare portrays love in this scene.'

▼ This photograph is from a 2012 production that used modern dress. Discuss how successful you think this is. What are the advantages of setting Shakespeare in different time periods rather than remaining faithful to traditional costumes? Talk through your ideas with a partner.

latched captured, mastered

of force she must be eyed he must see her

Stand close (so they cannot be seen)

rebuke tell off

chide scold, reprimand,

Being o'er shoes in blood having gone so far

be bored have a hole made through it

noontide midday

dead pale as death

Venus in Roman mythology, the goddess of love

carcass body

I led them on in this distracted fear,
And left sweet Pyramus translated there;
When in that moment, so it came to pass,
Titania waked, and straightway loved an ass.

OBERON This falls out better than I could devise.
But hast thou yet latched the Athenian's eyes
With the love juice, as I did bid thee do?

PUCK I took him sleeping – that is finished too –
And the Athenian woman by his side,
That when he waked, of force she must be eyed.

Enter DEMETRIUS *and* HERMIA.

OBERON Stand close: this is the same Athenian.

PUCK This is the woman, but not this the man.

DEMETRIUS O, why rebuke you him that loves you so?
Lay breath so bitter on your bitter foe.

HERMIA Now I but chide; but I should use thee worse,
For thou, I fear, hast given me cause to curse.
If thou hast slain Lysander in his sleep,
Being o'er shoes in blood, plunge in the deep,
And kill me too.
The sun was not so true unto the day
As he to me. Would he have stol'n away
From sleeping Hermia? I'll believe as soon
This whole earth may be bored, and that the moon
May through the centre creep, and so displease
Her brother's noontide with th'Antipodes.
It cannot be but thou hast murdered him:
So should a murderer look; so dead, so grim.

DEMETRIUS So should the murdered look, and so should I,
Pierced through the heart with your stern cruelty;
Yet you, the murderer, look as bright, as clear,
As yonder Venus in her glimmering sphere.

HERMIA What's this to my Lysander? Where is he?
Ah, good Demetrius, wilt thou give him me?

DEMETRIUS I had rather give his carcass to my hounds.

Hermia storms off, after accusing Demetrius of murder. Demetrius, too tired to follow, goes to sleep. Oberon tells Puck to find Helena in order to correct his mistake.

1 Getting to know the lovers (in pairs)

Shakespeare presents distinct views of the world through the different groups in the play (such as the lovers and fairies). Each character in these groups also has their own opinions, such as Hermia and Demetrius here.

a Go through lines 43–81 in your pair. One person makes notes on what Hermia thinks is going on here, the other on what Demetrius thinks.

b Share your ideas and compare the thoughts of the two lovers. Suggest similarities to and differences from the encounter between Lysander and Hermia in Act 2 Scene 2, lines 41–71.

Characters

Oberon – different intentions?

a Read Oberon's two speeches in the script opposite. Write a paragraph on what the lines tell you about this character and his motives in dealing with the mortals.

b Compare these speeches with those of Oberon in Act 2, particularly between lines 146–87 in Scene 1.

c Write a further paragraph comparing Oberon's motives with his treatment of his wife. Think about his words here in Act 3 Scene 2, lines 96–7: 'All fancy-sick she is and pale of cheer / With sighs of love, that costs the fresh blood dear.' Consider also his threat in Act 2 Scene 1, lines 146–7: 'Well, go thy way. Thou shalt not from this grove / Til I torment thee for this injury.'

2 Are men fickle? (in pairs)

Puck says 'one man holding troth, / A million fail' (see note in glossary on this page). Debate whether men are fickle in love, and, if so, whether they are more fickle than women. Make notes to prepare for a group discussion.

Stagecraft

'look how I go!'

I go, I go, look how I go!
Swifter than arrow from the Tartar's bow.

Suggest how the actor playing Puck should leave the stage here.

cur coward

Henceforth from this moment on

Durst thou dare you

worm snake

doubler tongue more forked, more deceitful

misprised mistaken

heaviness weariness

tender payment of a debt (i.e. he owes himself some sleep)

misprision mistake

perforce ensue must of necessity follow

Then fate … oath on oath so fate takes charge because for each man who is a faithful lover, a million fail, breaking their word time after time

fancy-sick sick with love

cheer face

Tartar central Asian warrior

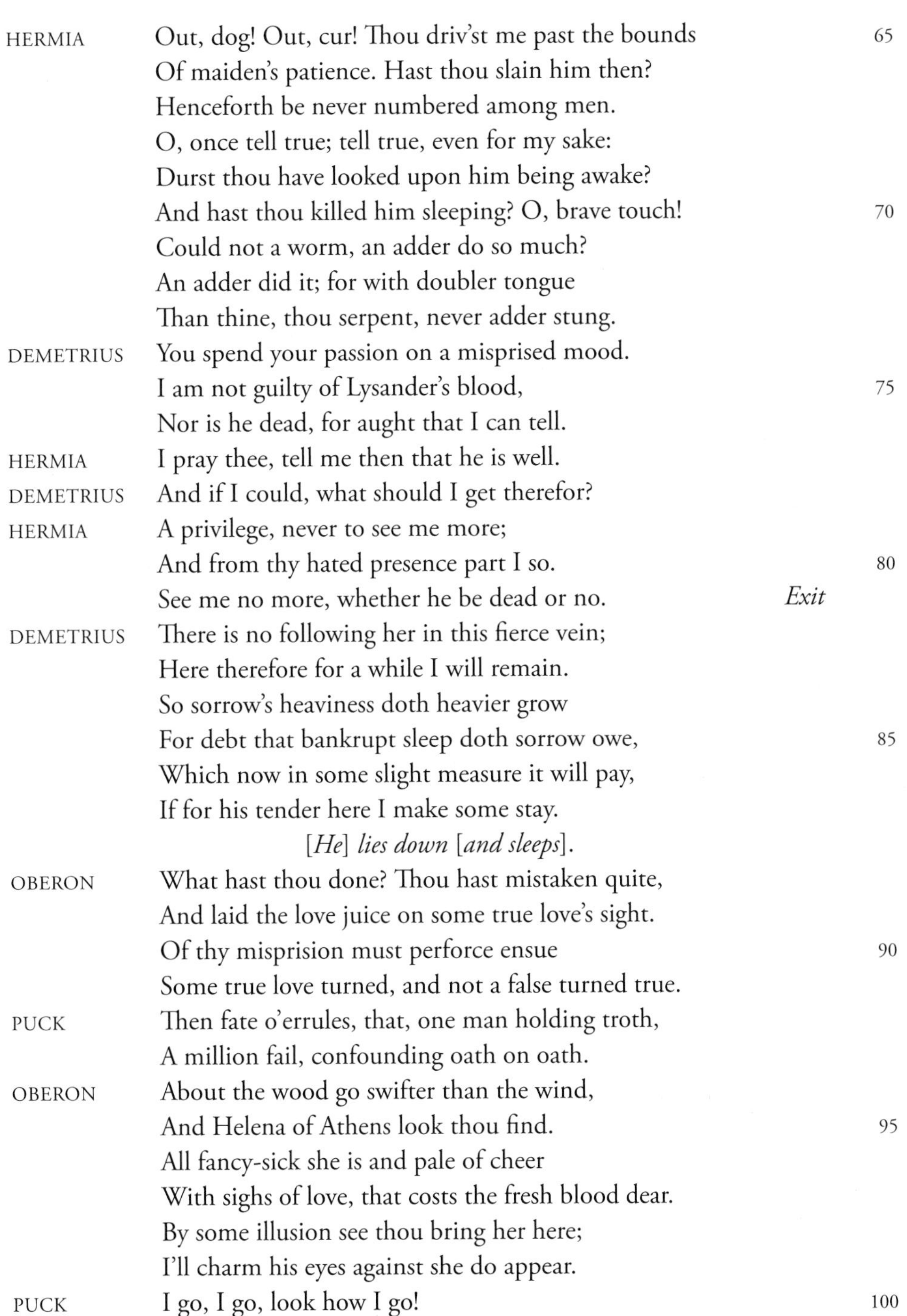

HERMIA Out, dog! Out, cur! Thou driv'st me past the bounds
Of maiden's patience. Hast thou slain him then?
Henceforth be never numbered among men.
O, once tell true; tell true, even for my sake:
Durst thou have looked upon him being awake?
And hast thou killed him sleeping? O, brave touch!
Could not a worm, an adder do so much?
An adder did it; for with doubler tongue
Than thine, thou serpent, never adder stung.

DEMETRIUS You spend your passion on a misprised mood.
I am not guilty of Lysander's blood,
Nor is he dead, for aught that I can tell.

HERMIA I pray thee, tell me then that he is well.

DEMETRIUS And if I could, what should I get therefor?

HERMIA A privilege, never to see me more;
And from thy hated presence part I so.
See me no more, whether he be dead or no. *Exit*

DEMETRIUS There is no following her in this fierce vein;
Here therefore for a while I will remain.
So sorrow's heaviness doth heavier grow
For debt that bankrupt sleep doth sorrow owe,
Which now in some slight measure it will pay,
If for his tender here I make some stay.

[*He*] *lies down* [*and sleeps*].

OBERON What hast thou done? Thou hast mistaken quite,
And laid the love juice on some true love's sight.
Of thy misprision must perforce ensue
Some true love turned, and not a false turned true.

PUCK Then fate o'errules, that, one man holding troth,
A million fail, confounding oath on oath.

OBERON About the wood go swifter than the wind,
And Helena of Athens look thou find.
All fancy-sick she is and pale of cheer
With sighs of love, that costs the fresh blood dear.
By some illusion see thou bring her here;
I'll charm his eyes against she do appear.

PUCK I go, I go, look how I go!
Swifter than arrow from the Tartar's bow. *Exit*

Oberon puts the magic juice on Demetrius's eyes, and Lysander enters with Helena. He is still trying to convince Helena that he loves her. She thinks he's lying.

1 Puck – a child?

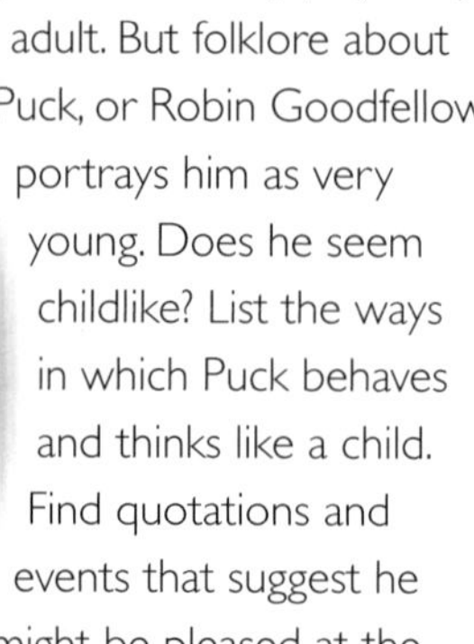

Today, Puck is usually played by an adult. But folklore about Puck, or Robin Goodfellow, portrays him as very young. Does he seem childlike? List the ways in which Puck behaves and thinks like a child. Find quotations and events that suggest he might be pleased at the mayhem and be insensitive to the feelings of the lovers.

Themes

'Lord, what fools these mortals be!' (in small groups)

Here, the audience laughs along with Puck at 'mortals' like the lovers. Are human beings fools? In what ways?

Place a large sheet of paper in the centre of your group. Together, suggest moments so far in the play where mortals have been shown behaving or speaking foolishly, and write them on the paper. Everyone should contribute. Each group decides on the best ideas and shares them with the class.

2 Class direction (whole class)

You need three volunteers – one to play Puck, one to play Oberon and one the sleeping Demetrius. The class directs the actors through lines 88–121. Take all suggestions seriously, try them and evaluate them. Think about:

• showing relationships • movement • gestures • tone of voice • use of silence • emphasis on particular words • creating dramatic effect

See if you can reach a unanimous decision about what works best as a vision of the characters in this episode. To work, this exercise needs imagination, confidence and, most importantly, respectful listening skills.

apple pupil

fee reward

fond pageant foolish scene

befall prepost'rously turn out absurdly and unnaturally

vow promise

nativity birth/delivery

badge of faith tears

truth … fray! Lysander's new 'truth' destroys the 'truth' of his promises to Hermia ('holy' involves vows of devotion, 'devilish' is a false vow)

light as tales containing as much truth as stories (i.e. none)

OBERON [*Squeezing the juice on Demetrius's eyes.*]
Flower of this purple dye,
Hit with Cupid's archery,
Sink in apple of his eye.
When his love he doth espy,
Let her shine as gloriously
As the Venus of the sky.
When thou wak'st, if she be by,
Beg of her for remedy.

Enter Puck.

PUCK Captain of our fairy band,
Helena is here at hand,
And the youth mistook by me,
Pleading for a lover's fee.
Shall we their fond pageant see?
Lord, what fools these mortals be!

OBERON Stand aside. The noise they make
Will cause Demetrius to awake.

PUCK Then will two at once woo one –
That must needs be sport alone;
And those things do best please me
That befall prepost'rously.

Enter LYSANDER *and* HELENA.

LYSANDER Why should you think that I should woo in scorn?
Scorn and derision never come in tears.
Look when I vow, I weep; and vows so born,
In their nativity all truth appears.
How can these things in me seem scorn to you,
Bearing the badge of faith to prove them true?

HELENA You do advance your cunning more and more.
When truth kills truth, O devilish-holy fray!
These vows are Hermia's. Will you give her o'er?
Weigh oath with oath, and you will nothing weigh;
Your vows to her and me, put in two scales,
Will even weigh, and both as light as tales.

LYSANDER I had no judgement when to her I swore.

Demetrius wakes, and tells Helena in very exaggerated language how much he loves her. She thinks that he is part of the plot to mock her.

Characters

Demetrius's transformation

Remind yourself of Demetrius's language and behaviour towards Helena so far in the play.

a Find three quotations that sum up his character and his feelings for Helena prior to waking under the influence of the potion.

b Now choose three quotations that show his transformation upon waking.

If you would like to reflect more on this, see 'Demetrius', page 160.

◀ **Notice Puck's and Oberon's expressions. What might they be thinking as they watch Helena, Demetrius and Lysander?**

Write about it

Helena's changing emotions

Read Helena's speech in the script opposite carefully. Reveal Helena's changing emotions and her developing character by writing down her thoughts and feelings in modern prose using the first person.

1 The dance of the lovers – who loves whom? (III)

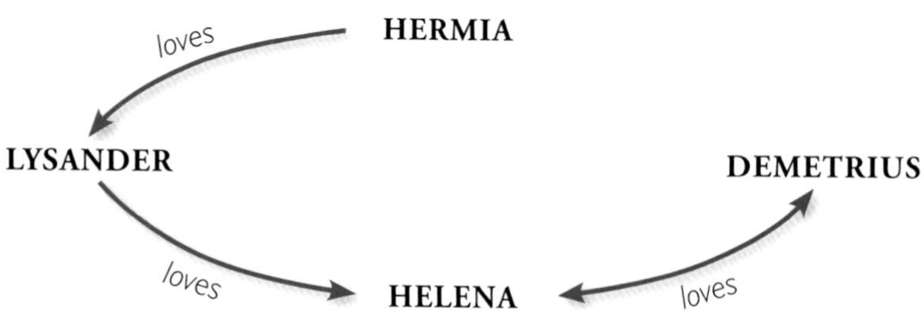

Taurus mountains in Turkey

courtesy courteous behaviour

join in souls work together whole-heartedly

trim neat, fine

noble sort good character

sport fun

HELENA Nor none, in my mind, now you give her o'er.
LYSANDER Demetrius loves her, and he loves not you.
DEMETRIUS (*Waking.*)
O Helen, goddess, nymph, perfect, divine!
To what, my love, shall I compare thine eyne?
Crystal is muddy! O, how ripe in show
Thy lips, those kissing cherries, tempting grow!
That pure congealèd white, high Taurus' snow,
Fanned with the eastern wind, turns to a crow
When thou hold'st up thy hand. O, let me kiss
This princess of pure white, this seal of bliss!
HELENA O spite! O Hell! I see you all are bent
To set against me for your merriment.
If you were civil, and knew courtesy,
You would not do me thus much injury.
Can you not hate me, as I know you do,
But you must join in souls to mock me too?
If you were men, as men you are in show,
You would not use a gentle lady so,
To vow, and swear, and superpraise my parts,
When I am sure you hate me with your hearts.
You both are rivals, and love Hermia;
And now both rivals to mock Helena.
A trim exploit, a manly enterprise,
To conjure tears up in a poor maid's eyes
With your derision! None of noble sort
Would so offend a virgin, and extort
A poor soul's patience, all to make you sport.

Lysander and Demetrius argue over Helena. Hermia enters and asks Lysander why he left her. Lysander replies it is because he hates her.

1 The lovers at war

Remember that the two men are under the influence of the flower's magic, but the two women do not suffer the same enchantment; they are bewildered by what's going on.

a Keep this difference between the state of the men and that of the women in mind as you read or act out the rest of the scene.

b Look carefully at the photos on this and the previous page, and consider how the actors in the two productions are revealing their state of mind.

Stagecraft

Onlookers – or voyeurs? (in small groups)

When you read the lovers' developing quarrels it is easy to forget that Puck and Oberon are also on stage watching, although when you see a performance their presence is always obvious. This kind of voyeurism – watching the pain and confusion of others – does not reflect well on them. But are Puck and Oberon simply voyeurs?

a Explore the involvement and responses of Puck and Oberon. Should they move or stay still? Should they exchange glances with each other and/or with the audience? Draw up a list of suggestions and try them out in your group.

b How can you make it clear to an audience who is visible and who is invisible? In the production pictured below, Puck and Oberon are positioned high out of the lovers' sightline. In another, the colour of their costumes allowed them to melt into the background. In a third, Oberon and Puck wore luminous cloaks to indicate their magic invisibility. What would you do? Discuss this in your groups, and sketch some of your ideas.

yield you up give you

bequeath give

guest-wise sojourned stayed for a while, like a visitor

Disparage speak badly of

Lest unless

aby pay for

apprehension understanding

recompense compensation

bide stay

engilds the night gives the night a golden sheen

oes bright dress ornaments (or stars)

LYSANDER You are unkind, Demetrius: be not so,
For you love Hermia – this you know I know –
And here with all good will, with all my heart,
In Hermia's love I yield you up my part;
And yours of Helena to me bequeath,
Whom I do love, and will do till my death.

HELENA Never did mockers waste more idle breath.

DEMETRIUS Lysander, keep thy Hermia; I will none.
If e'er I loved her, all that love is gone.
My heart to her but as guest-wise sojourned,
And now to Helen is it home returned,
There to remain.

LYSANDER Helen, it is not so.

DEMETRIUS Disparage not the faith thou dost not know,
Lest to thy peril thou aby it dear.
Look where thy love comes: yonder is thy dear.

Enter Hermia.

HERMIA Dark night, that from the eye his function takes,
The ear more quick of apprehension makes;
Wherein it doth impair the seeing sense
It pays the hearing double recompense.
Thou art not by mine eye, Lysander, found;
Mine ear, I thank it, brought me to thy sound.
But why unkindly didst thou leave me so?

LYSANDER Why should he stay whom love doth press to go?

HERMIA What love could press Lysander from my side?

LYSANDER Lysander's love, that would not let him bide,
Fair Helena – who more engilds the night
Than all yon fiery oes and eyes of light.
[*To Hermia*] Why seek'st thou me? Could not this make thee know
The hate I bare thee made me leave thee so?

HERMIA You speak not as you think; it cannot be.

Helena now thinks everyone is mocking her, and complains that Hermia should behave better as they have been such close friends for so long.

▲ The lovers, watched intently by Puck and Oberon. Which line do you think is being spoken at this moment?

confederacy plot
conjoined joined together
in spite of me to spite me
Injurious wrongful, harmful

bait torment
foul derision terrible mockery

chid scolded

artificial highly skilled

sampler piece of embroidery
warbling singing
in one key in harmony
incorporate united in one body

But yet an union in partition two parts of the same, like the partition on a coat of arms

rent tear

1 Helena's speech (in pairs)

a One of you reads Helena's speech aloud. During this, the other person notes down the words and phrases that dominate and/or resonate most strongly with them.

b Swap roles and repeat the activity.

c Now compare what you have written down. Prioritise the most important ideas for you both. Together, construct one sentence describing the most important ideas communicated by this speech.

2 Sisterhood under pressure (in small groups)

Helena's speech raises the issue of loyalty between women. Discuss whether you think falling in love always puts a strain on female friendships. Share your ideas on what emotions you think the female characters feel here. Then consider if those same feelings are present in female relationships today – and whether it is the same for men.

HELENA Lo, she is one of this confederacy!
Now I perceive they have conjoined all three
To fashion this false sport in spite of me.
Injurious Hermia, most ungrateful maid,
Have you conspired, have you with these contrived
To bait me with this foul derision?
Is all the counsel that we two have shared,
The sisters' vows, the hours that we have spent
When we have chid the hasty-footed time
For parting us – O, is all forgot?
All schooldays' friendship, childhood innocence?
We, Hermia, like two artificial gods
Have with our needles created both one flower,
Both on one sampler, sitting on one cushion,
Both warbling of one song, both in one key,
As if our hands, our sides, voices, and minds
Had been incorporate. So we grew together
Like to a double cherry, seeming parted,
But yet an union in partition,
Two lovely berries moulded on one stem;
So with two seeming bodies but one heart,
Two of the first, like coats in heraldry,
Due but to one, and crownèd with one crest.
And will you rent our ancient love asunder,
To join with men in scorning your poor friend?
It is not friendly, 'tis not maidenly.
Our sex, as well as I, may chide you for it,
Though I alone do feel the injury.

HERMIA I am amazèd at your passionate words.
I scorn you not; it seems that you scorn me.

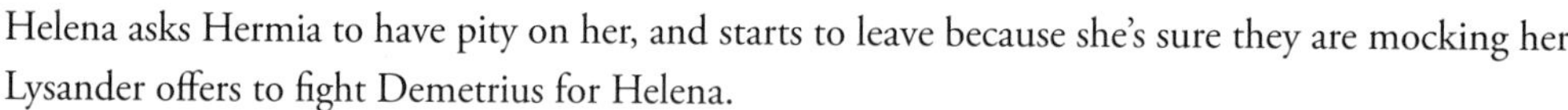

Helena asks Hermia to have pity on her, and starts to leave because she's sure they are mocking her. Lysander offers to fight Demetrius for Helena.

1 Helena's bewilderment and distress (in pairs)

Helena, thoroughly confused by what is going on, makes three long speeches.

a Her first speech, lines 192–219, stresses the great friendship she and Hermia have always enjoyed. Work through it, identifying all the images of positive relationships and childhood. Which image strikes you as most powerfully conveying close friendship? Explain why.

b In her second speech, lines 222–35, she accuses Hermia of encouraging the two men to mock her, and appeals for pity. Take turns to speak the lines, bringing out Helena's accusatory tone as strongly as you can by stressing the words that most express her feelings.

c Her third speech, lines 237–44, is spoken to all three of the other characters. She accuses them all of laughing at her, condemns them for making her the subject of their 'sport', and prepares to leave, blaming herself. By this time Helena is probably very emotional and may accompany all she says with gestures and facial expressions. Speak the lines, using actions to illustrate their meaning.

Themes

Men fighting over women (in pairs)

In lines 248–56, the men begin to quarrel and they resort to threats of violence – 'withdraw and prove it too'. The lines suggest a rather conventional response and clearly mirror other scenes of male domination and aggression. The language seems to indicate that things are getting out of control. Before you read on, briefly predict some of the ways in which this conflict could end.

spurn me reject me
celestial heavenly
Wherefore why

tender me offer me
in grace in favour

Persever persevere, continue
counterfeit pretend
sad serious
Make mouths pull faces
chronicled told (as a funny story)
argument subject (for making fun of)
fare ye well goodbye

entreat plead
compel force

HELENA Have you not set Lysander, as in scorn,
To follow me, and praise my eyes and face?
And made your other love, Demetrius,
Who even but now did spurn me with his foot,
To call me goddess, nymph, divine and rare,
Precious, celestial? Wherefore speaks he this
To her he hates? And wherefore doth Lysander
Deny your love, so rich within his soul,
And tender me, forsooth, affection,
But by your setting on, by your consent?
What though I be not so in grace as you,
So hung upon with love, so fortunate,
But miserable most, to love unloved:
This you should pity rather than despise.

HERMIA I understand not what you mean by this.

HELENA Ay, do! Persever, counterfeit sad looks,
Make mouths upon me when I turn my back,
Wink each at other, hold the sweet jest up.
This sport, well carried, shall be chronicled.
If you have any pity, grace, or manners,
You would not make me such an argument.
But fare ye well. 'Tis partly my own fault,
Which death or absence soon shall remedy.

LYSANDER Stay, gentle Helena: hear my excuse,
My love, my life, my soul, fair Helena!

HELENA O, excellent!

HERMIA [*To Lysander*] Sweet, do not scorn her so.

DEMETRIUS If she cannot entreat, I can compel.

LYSANDER Thou canst compel no more than she entreat;
Thy threats have no more strength than her weak prayers.
Helen, I love thee, by my life, I do:
I swear by that which I will lose for thee
To prove him false that says I love thee not.

DEMETRIUS I say I love thee more than he can do.

LYSANDER If thou say so, withdraw, and prove it too.

DEMETRIUS Quick, come.

Hermia clings on to Lysander as he insults her and tells her that he hates her and loves Helena.

1 The quarrel – a read-through (in fours)

The quarrel between the lovers really heats up here. The episode provides wonderful entertainment in the theatre because, although it might seem serious, it usually comes over as very funny with lots of physical humour. **Dramatic irony** (when the audience knows something the characters do not) also plays a big part of the audience's amused response, as we are the only ones who know what is truly going on. To gain a first impression of what happens, take parts and read lines 256–344.

Write about it

Lysander's insults

Lysander's insults – 'Ethiop' and 'tawny Tartar' (references to Hermia's dark hair and complexion) – sound uncomfortable to modern ears. We are now sensitive to racist abuse in a way that the Elizabethans were not. In addition, in Shakespeare's time a tan was considered to be unladylike and to look weather-beaten. Ladies didn't walk much in the open air – it was the working people who had to be out in all weathers.

If you were directing a production, would you omit these insults? Write a few sentences giving the reasons for your decision.

2 Hermia's puzzlement – all questions (in pairs)

Now it is Hermia's turn to be bewildered by what is happening. She simply cannot understand why Lysander rejects and insults her. Most of what she says in the script opposite is in the form of questions.

Count the number of questions and analyse each one. Discuss why Shakespeare gives Hermia so many questions here. Suggest how you might answer her.

whereto tends all this? what do you mean?

Ethiop person from Ethiopia

tame lacking in spirit

burr prickly seed-case of a plant

tawny Tartar brown and ferocious person

bond oath, legal agreement

weak bond (Hermia's arms; also a reference to the weakness of Lysander's promises)

erewhile recently

In earnest seriously

HERMIA Lysander, whereto tends all this?
LYSANDER Away, you Ethiop!
DEMETRIUS No, no, sir,
Seem to break loose, take on as you would follow,
But yet come not. You are a tame man, go.
LYSANDER Hang off, thou cat, thou burr! Vile thing, let loose,
Or I will shake thee from me like a serpent.
HERMIA Why are you grown so rude? What change is this,
Sweet love?
LYSANDER Thy love? – out, tawny Tartar, out;
Out, loathed medicine! O hated potion, hence!
HERMIA Do you not jest?
HELENA Yes, sooth, and so do you.
LYSANDER Demetrius, I will keep my word with thee.
DEMETRIUS I would I had your bond, for I perceive
A weak bond holds you. I'll not trust your word.
LYSANDER What? Should I hurt her, strike her, kill her dead?
Although I hate her, I'll not harm her so.
HERMIA What? Can you do me greater harm than hate?
Hate me? Wherefore? O me, what news, my love?
Am not I Hermia? Are not you Lysander?
I am as fair now as I was erewhile.
Since night you loved me; yet since night you left me.
Why then, you left me – O, the gods forbid! –
In earnest, shall I say?
LYSANDER Ay, by my life;
And never did desire to see thee more.
Therefore be out of hope, of question, of doubt;
Be certain, nothing truer – 'tis no jest
That I do hate thee and love Helena.

Hermia turns on Helena and threatens to fight her, thinking Helena has stolen Lysander's love. Helena says she will return to Athens.

Stagecraft

Quarrels, insults and fights (in fours)

Hermia's puzzlement now turns to anger and she directs her rage at Helena, accusing her of having stolen Lysander's love. Hermia's accusations arouse Helena's indignation, and she responds with similar passion (notice again how Shakespeare shows that 'reason and love keep little company'). Anger leads to insults and insults to violence.

The two women seem very close to fighting, and in line 303 Helena says 'Let her not strike me'. Most directors create a very physical scene here. How would you stage this? In your group, come up with some ideas and try them out. Look at the images on this page and on page 88 to get you started. Record your ideas in your Director's Journal.

▼ Demetrius and Lysander holding back Hermia.

Characters

Love conceals, anger reveals

In previous scenes, we have witnessed a strong friendship between Hermia and Helena. Here, their characters and their relationship appear more complex. Write down evidence of how their relationship has changed. Use your ideas to construct a paragraph that explores this scene and what it reveals about the characters of both women.

canker-blossom diseased flower

i'faith truly

bashfulness shyness

counterfeit cheat

prevailed with him won Lysander's love

painted maypole tall thin pole around which people dance on May Day

curst fierce

shrewishness anger, scolding

maid for my cowardice cowardly young woman

simple uncomplicated

fond loving

HERMIA [*To Helena*]
O me, you juggler, you canker-blossom,
You thief of love! What, have you come by night
And stol'n my love's heart from him?

HELENA Fine, i'faith!
Have you no modesty, no maiden shame,
No touch of bashfulness? What, will you tear
Impatient answers from my gentle tongue?
Fie, fie, you counterfeit, you puppet, you!

HERMIA 'Puppet'? Why so? – Ay, that way goes the game.
Now I perceive that she hath made compare
Between our statures; she hath urged her height,
And with her personage, her tall personage,
Her height, forsooth, she hath prevailed with him.
And are you grown so high in his esteem
Because I am so dwarfish and so low?
How low am I, thou painted maypole? Speak!
How low am I? I am not yet so low
But that my nails can reach unto thine eyes.

HELENA I pray you, though you mock me, gentlemen,
Let her not hurt me. I was never curst;
I have no gift at all in shrewishness.
I am a right maid for my cowardice;
Let her not strike me. You perhaps may think
Because she is something lower than myself
That I can match her.

HERMIA Lower? Hark, again!

HELENA Good Hermia, do not be so bitter with me.
I evermore did love you, Hermia,
Did ever keep your counsels, never wronged you,
Save that in love unto Demetrius
I told him of your stealth unto this wood.
He followed you; for love I followed him,
But he hath chid me hence, and threatened me
To strike me, spurn me, nay, to kill me too.
And now, so you will let me quiet go,
To Athens will I bear my folly back,
And follow you no further. Let me go;
You see how simple and how fond I am.

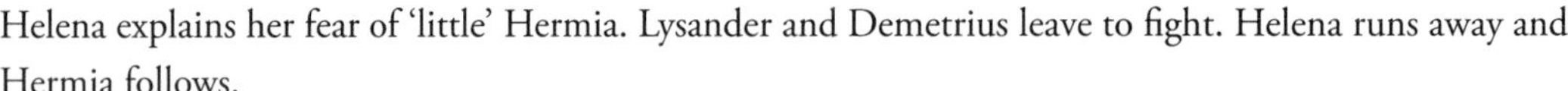

Helena explains her fear of 'little' Hermia. Lysander and Demetrius leave to fight. Helena runs away and Hermia follows.

Language in the play

Insults – 'You bead, you acorn' (in small groups)

a In your group, make a list of all the insults in the script opposite. Each person should then choose their two favourites. Take turns to shout them at each other. Add gestures and facial expressions to increase their impact.

b These insults now sound old-fashioned, but are there any that you would recommend bringing back? Why?

1 Storyboard

Act 3 Scene 2 is a long and complex scene, and it is easy to lose track of the order of events. Create a six-frame storyboard of the action in the lovers' story in this scene, up to the point of Hermia's exit. Place a caption or quotation in each frame that you feel best summarises the key moment in the scene.

shrewd vicious

flout me abuse me

minimus insignificant creature

knot-grass a weed that was thought to stunt growth

cheek by jowl face to face

coil turmoil

'long of because of

curst company awful presence

fray fight

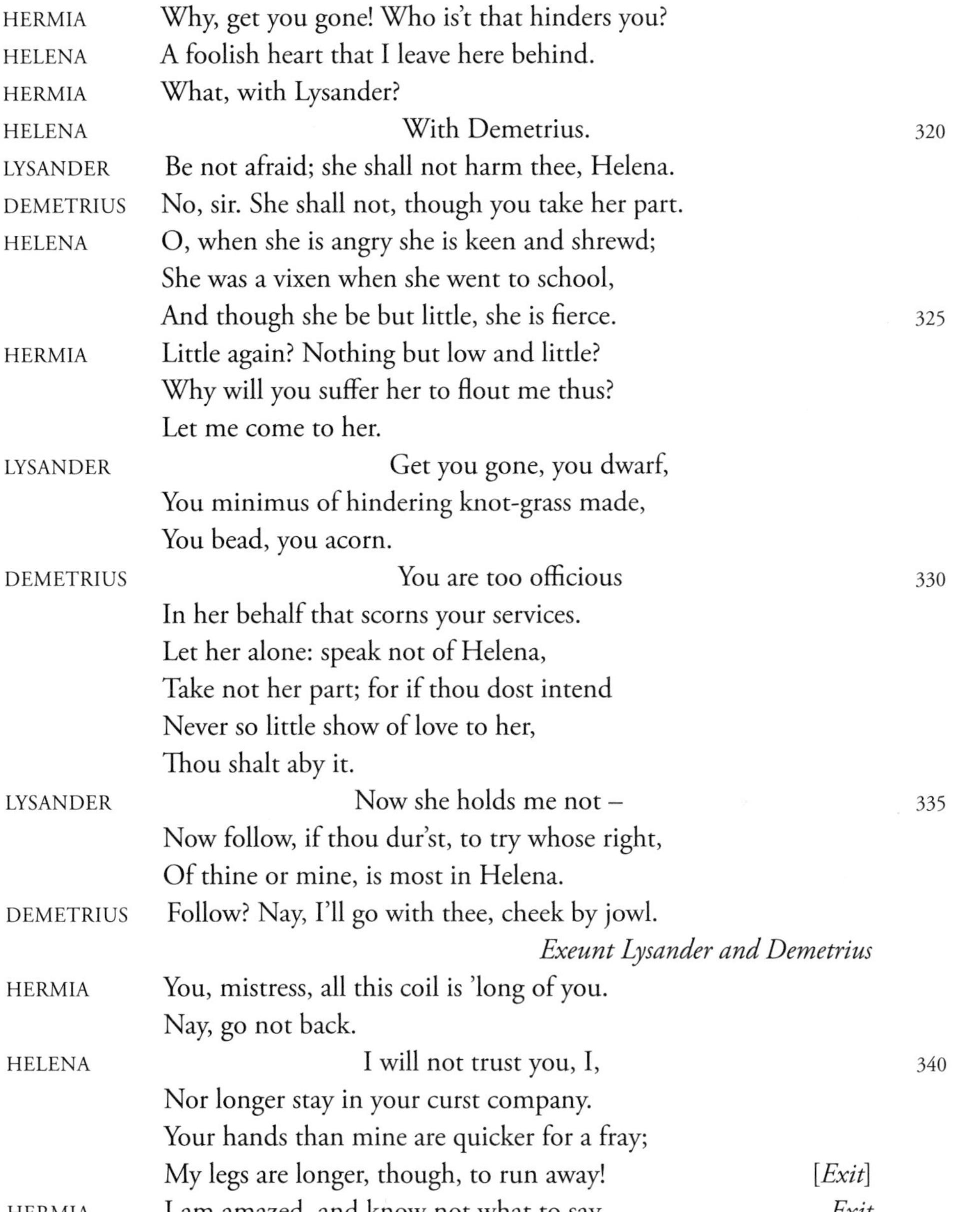

HERMIA Why, get you gone! Who is't that hinders you?
HELENA A foolish heart that I leave here behind.
HERMIA What, with Lysander?
HELENA With Demetrius.
LYSANDER Be not afraid; she shall not harm thee, Helena.
DEMETRIUS No, sir. She shall not, though you take her part.
HELENA O, when she is angry she is keen and shrewd;
She was a vixen when she went to school,
And though she be but little, she is fierce.
HERMIA Little again? Nothing but low and little?
Why will you suffer her to flout me thus?
Let me come to her.
LYSANDER Get you gone, you dwarf,
You minimus of hindering knot-grass made,
You bead, you acorn.
DEMETRIUS You are too officious
In her behalf that scorns your services.
Let her alone: speak not of Helena,
Take not her part; for if thou dost intend
Never so little show of love to her,
Thou shalt aby it.
LYSANDER Now she holds me not –
Now follow, if thou dur'st, to try whose right,
Of thine or mine, is most in Helena.
DEMETRIUS Follow? Nay, I'll go with thee, cheek by jowl.
Exeunt Lysander and Demetrius
HERMIA You, mistress, all this coil is 'long of you.
Nay, go not back.
HELENA I will not trust you, I,
Nor longer stay in your curst company.
Your hands than mine are quicker for a fray;
My legs are longer, though, to run away! [*Exit*]
HERMIA I am amazed, and know not what to say. *Exit*

Puck explains his mistake. Oberon orders him to lead Lysander and Demetrius astray by imitating their voices. He will 'beg' the boy from Titania, then release her from the charm and put all things right.

Stagecraft

Master and servant (in pairs)

a Talk together about how, in performance, you would show the relationship between Oberon and Puck here.

b During a long speech, the other actor on stage has the problem of reacting but saying nothing. Take turns to speak Oberon's lines in the script opposite while the other responds as Puck. His responses can be as subtle or as physical as you wish. Choose your favourite reaction and share it with the class.

1 Oberon the peacemaker

a Consider the photograph below and the one on page 92. What do they suggest about Oberon's qualities and whether he really wishes to bring about love and harmony? Use evidence from the script opposite to support your views.

b Oberon's power over others is clear in his speech here. Sum up in your own words exactly how he intends to put things right.

Themes

Waking from a dream

Oberon suggests that when the lovers wake, 'all this derision / Shall seem a dream and fruitless vision'.

How might the audience react to the suggestion that everything that has happened is just a dream, a kind of surreal parallel universe?

sort turn out

jangling discord and disorder

welkin sky

Acheron one of the rivers in Hades, the underworld for the dead

testy bad-tempered

Like … frame thy tongue deceive by imitating Lysander

bitter wrong sharp accusations

rail use abusive language

death-counterfeiting sleep sleep like the dead

leaden heavy

wonted usual

derision stupidity

fruitless useless, pointless

wend make their way

league contract, agreement

date duration

Oberon and Puck come forward.

OBERON This is thy negligence. Still thou mistak'st,
Or else committ'st thy knaveries wilfully.

PUCK Believe me, King of Shadows, I mistook.
Did not you tell me I should know the man
By the Athenian garments he had on?
And so far blameless proves my enterprise
That I have 'nointed an Athenian's eyes;
And so far am I glad it so did sort,
As this their jangling I esteem a sport.

OBERON Thou seest these lovers seek a place to fight:
Hie therefore, Robin, overcast the night;
The starry welkin cover thou anon
With drooping fog as black as Acheron,
And lead these testy rivals so astray
As one come not within another's way.
Like to Lysander sometime frame thy tongue,
Then stir Demetrius up with bitter wrong,
And sometime rail thou like Demetrius;
And from each other look thou lead them thus,
Till o'er their brows death-counterfeiting sleep
With leaden legs and batty wings doth creep.
Then crush this herb into Lysander's eye,
Whose liquor hath this virtuous property,
To take from thence all error with his might,
And make his eyeballs roll with wonted sight.
When they next wake, all this derision
Shall seem a dream and fruitless vision,
And back to Athens shall the lovers wend
With league whose date till death shall never end.
Whiles I in this affair do thee employ
I'll to my Queen and beg her Indian boy;
And then I will her charmèd eye release
From monster's view, and all things shall be peace.

Day approaches, and though the fairies (unlike other spirits) can exist in the day, Oberon urges haste. Puck looks forward to misleading the lovers. Lysander returns and Puck deceives him.

▼ Why do you think the director of this production has chosen to portray Oberon and Puck in this way?

Language in the play

Puck's and Oberon's language (in pairs)

a With your partner, focus on either Puck's or Oberon's speech and explore what you find interesting and powerful in their imagery and diction. What picture of each character and of the fairy world is being painted here, and to what effect?

b Move to sit with someone who has considered the other character. In turn, talk through your ideas. Ask questions if there is anything you don't understand about your partner's ideas.

Write about it

Images of the fairy world (by yourself)

Spend fifteen minutes writing a response to the following statement: 'The language of the fairy world is full of intense and memorable imagery.' Use quotations from this scene to support your ideas and opinions.

Aurora's harbinger morning star, announcing the arrival of the dawn goddess

aye ever

consort keep company

forester man who looks after game and guards against poachers

grove may tread can walk in the woods

Neptune god of the sea; the morning sun's beams transform the sea from green to 'yellow gold'

notwithstanding in spite of

drawn with drawn sword

plainer more open

PUCK My fairy lord, this must be done with haste,
For night's swift dragons cut the clouds full fast,
And yonder shines Aurora's harbinger,
At whose approach ghosts wandering here and there
Troop home to churchyards. Damnèd spirits all,
That in crossways and floods have burial,
Already to their wormy beds are gone.
For fear lest day should look their shames upon,
They wilfully themselves exile from light,
And must for aye consort with black-browed night.

OBERON But we are spirits of another sort.
I with the morning's love have oft made sport,
And like a forester the groves may tread
Even till the eastern gate, all fiery-red,
Opening on Neptune with fair blessèd beams,
Turns into yellow gold his salt green streams.
But notwithstanding, haste, make no delay;
We may effect this business yet ere day. [*Exit*]

PUCK Up and down, up and down,
I will lead them up and down;
I am feared in field and town.
Goblin, lead them up and down.
Here comes one.

Enter Lysander.

LYSANDER Where art thou, proud Demetrius? Speak thou now.

PUCK Here, villain, drawn and ready! Where art thou?

LYSANDER I will be with thee straight.

PUCK Follow me then
To plainer ground.

[*Exit Lysander*]

Puck misleads both Demetrius and Lysander by imitating their voices. Both men finally have had enough and fall asleep.

Stagecraft

Four practical problems to resolve (in small groups)

a Consider how Puck should imitate Lysander's voice well enough to fool Demetrius (and, a little later, imitate Demetrius's own voice). Discuss the different dramatic effects of using good imitation and deliberately inaccurate imitation.

b It is meant to be as dark as 'black-browed night', so Lysander and Demetrius cannot see each other and become confused. How could this effect be achieved and yet still allow the audience to see the action clearly?

c Work out how to position the lovers near to one another. Remember that Lysander must sleep near Hermia, so that he falls back in love with her when he wakes. The stage direction simply reads '*Sleeps*', but in many productions Puck takes a direct (and often very funny) part in getting the lovers to sleep near their intended partners.

d The characters in this play sleep a lot and this could cause practical problems on stage. If you were directing, would you want actors to lie on the bare stage floor, or would you want a set that offered more comfortable options such as mossy banks or grassy glades? Talk together about the problems and the solutions, and then sketch or write in your Director's Journal your ideas for a set that accommodates the sleeping lovers.

recreant coward, villain

defiled made dirty

manhood manliness (usually associated with strength and courage)

lighter-heeled faster

Abide face

wot know

buy this dear suffer, pay dearly

faintness constraineth me I am overcome by faintness

measure out my length lie down

Enter Demetrius.

DEMETRIUS Lysander, speak again.
Thou runaway, thou coward, art thou fled?
Speak! In some bush? Where dost thou hide thy head?

PUCK Thou coward, art thou bragging to the stars,
Telling the bushes that thou look'st for wars,
And wilt not come? Come, recreant, come, thou child,
I'll whip thee with a rod. He is defiled
That draws a sword on thee.

DEMETRIUS Yea, art thou there?

PUCK Follow my voice. We'll try no manhood here.

Exeunt

[*Enter Lysander.*]

LYSANDER He goes before me, and still dares me on;
When I come where he calls, then he is gone.
The villain is much lighter-heeled than I;
I followed fast, but faster he did fly,
That fallen am I in dark uneven way,
And here will rest me. (*Lies down.*) Come, thou gentle day,
For if but once thou show me thy grey light
I'll find Demetrius and revenge this spite. [*Sleeps.*]

Enter Puck and Demetrius.

PUCK Ho, ho, ho! Coward, why com'st thou not?

DEMETRIUS Abide me if thou dar'st, for well I wot
Thou runn'st before me, shifting every place,
And dar'st not stand nor look me in the face.
Where art thou now?

PUCK Come hither; I am here.

DEMETRIUS Nay then, thou mock'st me. Thou shalt buy this dear
If ever I thy face by daylight see.
Now, go thy way; faintness constraineth me
To measure out my length on this cold bed.
By day's approach look to be visited. [*Sleeps.*]

Helena and Hermia enter separately, exhausted, and fall asleep. Puck puts the magic juice on Lysander's eyes to make him love Hermia again.

Language in the play

Rhymes – mortals and fairies (in threes)

The final two episodes of this scene (from line 350) are in rhyming verse. The rhymes are particularly obvious in the script opposite. In Shakespeare's day, 'east' could rhyme with 'detest'.

Take parts and read aloud the script opposite, emphasising the rhymes. Then talk together about whether Puck (a fairy) can more convincingly stress the rhymes than Hermia and Helena (mortals). What would be your advice to the actors?

Write about it

Sleep and dreams

At the end of the scene, the lovers are asleep. Write down the thoughts and feelings of each as they drift into sleep. Use rhyming couplets if you dare! Alternatively, write about their dreams.

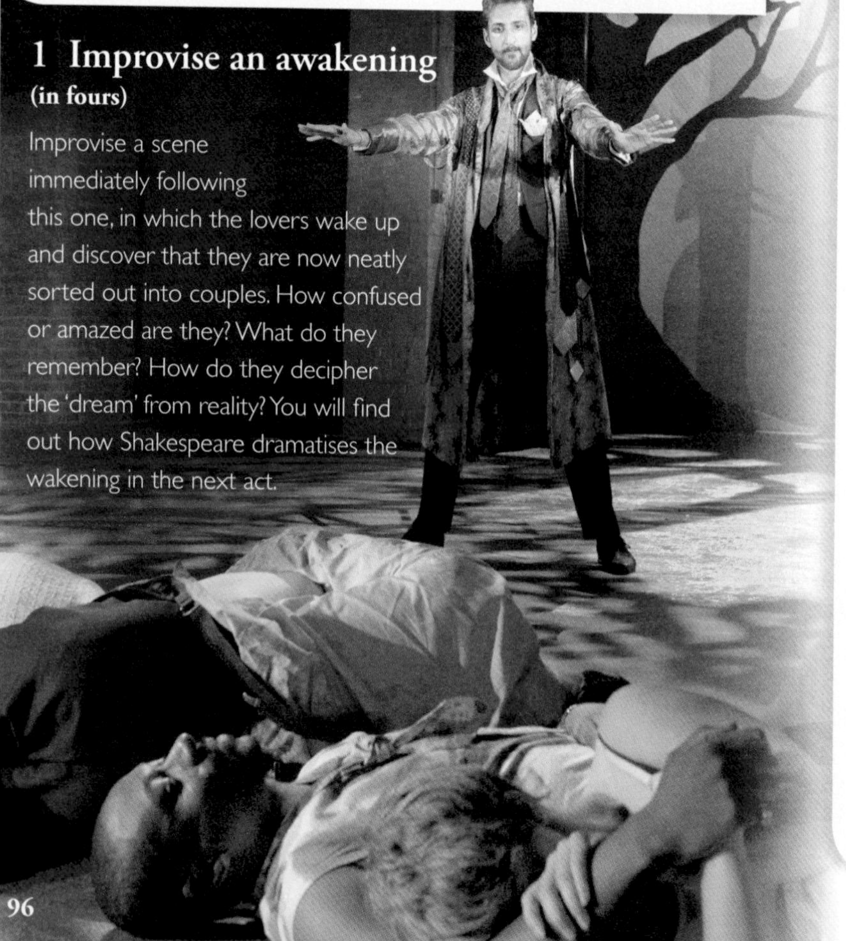

1 Improvise an awakening (in fours)

Improvise a scene immediately following this one, in which the lovers wake up and discover that they are now neatly sorted out into couples. How confused or amazed are they? What do they remember? How do they decipher the 'dream' from reality? You will find out how Shakespeare dramatises the wakening in the next act.

Abate diminish, cut short

curst bad-tempered

Bedabbled stained

briars prickly bush

Jack shall have Jill … The man shall have his mare again proverbs of Shakespeare's time for 'boy gets girl'

Enter Helena.

HELENA O weary night, O long and tedious night,
Abate thy hours, shine comforts from the east,
That I may back to Athens by daylight
From these that my poor company detest;
And sleep, that sometimes shuts up sorrow's eye,
Steal me awhile from mine own company. (*Sleeps.*)

PUCK Yet but three? Come one more,
Two of both kinds makes up four.
Here she comes, curst and sad.
Cupid is a knavish lad
Thus to make poor females mad.

Enter Hermia.

HERMIA Never so weary, never so in woe,
Bedabbled with the dew, and torn with briars –
I can no further crawl, no further go;
My legs can keep no pace with my desires.
Here will I rest me till the break of day.
Heavens shield Lysander, if they mean a fray. [*Sleeps.*]

PUCK On the ground
Sleep sound.
I'll apply
To your eye,
Gentle lover, remedy.
[*Squeezes the juice on Lysander's eyes.*]
When thou wak'st,
Thou tak'st
True delight
In the sight
Of thy former lady's eye;
And the country proverb known,
That every man should take his own,
In your waking shall be shown.
Jack shall have Jill,
Naught shall go ill:
The man shall have his mare again, and all shall be well.
[*Exit Puck;*] *the lovers remain on stage, asleep*

Looking back at Act 3

Activities for groups or individuals

1 Transformation

There are many myths about people being transformed into animals, including asses (you may want to research this in both mythology and literature). Bottom is something of an ass (fool) already. Some people have seen a darker side to his transformation into a real ass, associating the ass with sexual prowess. Others see it as a mockery of romance and of both men and women's behaviour when in love.

Discuss with a partner the effect on the audience of including this transformation in the play. Share your ideas with the class.

2 The world of the wood

Creating a magical woodland on stage, where so much complex action and change occurs, is a significant undertaking for a set designer. Use one or more of the following activities to help you visualise the importance and impact of setting in the play.

- **a** **Map** Devise a map of Athens and the wood. The play hints at locations, but think about Titania's bower in relation to the Mechanicals' rehearsal space. Also insert where the various lovers' scenes might take place. (Remember that the Mechanicals don't meet the lovers.)
- **b** **Website** Design a website for 'a wood near Athens'. Your aim is to attract tourists.
- **c** **Mood board** Create a mood board (a poster that uses colours, images, textures and samples to present a design) to show how you think the world of the woods should look on stage. You could use drawings, photographs, paints, images from magazines or other productions, fabric samples and so on.
- **d** **Board game** Develop a board game based on *A Midsummer Night's Dream*.
- **e** **Stage set** For professional stage productions, designers always make a detailed model set before proceeding to the full-sized version. Sketch or describe in writing your own stage set for the woodland scenes.
- **f** **Costume design** Design costumes for the fairy world. In the play's imagery, fairies are connected with the natural world and the woodland. Use this connection to help your thinking about costume and colour. As you design costumes for the fairy world, think of contrasting dress for the Mechanicals, the lovers and the court.

3 Binary oppositions

A **binary opposition** is a pair of opposites commonly used in literature to compare ideas, values and language. Literature is full of comparisons and juxtapositions between ideas such as youth and age, innocence and experience and good and evil. A good example is the opposition of day and night, where night represents menace, danger and the unconscious, and is juxtaposed with day – a time of clarity, light and consciousness. Interesting binary oppositions in *A Midsummer Night's Dream* are the contrasting of the rational versus the emotional, and dreams versus reality.

In a group, make a list of as many binary opposites in the play as you can find. Which characters would you attach each of these to in particular? Try to find evidence in the script that supports your understanding of each of your opposites.

4 Stage directions

There is a lot of movement and action in Act 3, making it complex for actors to enter, exit, respond appropriately and position themselves on stage. Pick a part of this act that interests you, and rewrite the stage directions to give the actors more information and thus try to improve their performance.

▲ *The Nightmare* **by John Henry Fuseli, 1781.**

5 Midsummer dream – or nightmare?

There are many nightmarish things about this play – including Bottom being turned into an ass, and Hermia's nightmare of the snake.

Describe, paint or draw a memorable dream you have had. Then, in groups, relate your dreams and nightmares, and see if you can find meaning in them. Discuss whether you believe dreams have any significance to our lives, if they reveal our fears and if they can inform or influence reality.

Titania speaks lovingly to Bottom. He gives instructions to her fairies to scratch him and find him food.

Characters

Bottom (in sixes)

a With your group, discuss how you would portray Bottom here. During your discussion, consider the following questions:

- How aware is Bottom of what is happening? Is he puzzled or can he not believe his good fortune?
- Look again at the requests he makes of the fairies. What do you find interesting and amusing?
- What do we learn about Bottom's character? How does he view himself?
- What do you notice about his language (for example, note his **malapropisms** – the mistaken use of words that sound similar)? What do you think his tone would be as he talks to the fairies?

b Now practise acting out the scene up to line 99. Afterwards, perform your version to the class.

▲ **Bottom, Titania and the fairies. Talk with a partner about the mood that you think this production has created of the fairy world.**

coy caress

Mounsieur monsieur (Bottom is using poor French)

red-hipped humble-bee bumblebee

fret worry

overflown covered

neaf hand

leave your courtesy you don't need to bow

Cavalery a gentleman (Bottom's mistake for 'cavalier')

tender sensitive

tongs and the bones simple musical instruments, such as a triangle and castanets

a peck of provender a little food

bottle bundle

Act 4 Scene 1
The wood

Enter TITANIA, *Queen of Fairies, and* BOTTOM, *and fairies [including* PEASEBLOSSOM, COBWEB *and* MUSTARDSEED;*] and the King* OBERON *behind them.*

TITANIA Come, sit thee down upon this flowery bed
While I thy amiable cheeks do coy,
And stick musk-roses in thy sleek smooth head,
And kiss thy fair large ears, my gentle joy.

BOTTOM Where's Peaseblossom?

PEASEBLOSSOM Ready.

BOTTOM Scratch my head, Peaseblossom. Where's Mounsieur Cobweb?

COBWEB Ready.

BOTTOM Mounsieur Cobweb, good Mounsieur, get you your weapons in your hand, and kill me a red-hipped humble-bee on the top of a thistle; and, good Mounsieur, bring me the honey-bag. Do not fret yourself too much in the action, Mounsieur; and, good Mounsieur, have a care the honey-bag break not; I would be loath to have you overflown with a honey-bag, signior. Where's Mounsieur Mustardseed?

MUSTARDSEED Ready.

BOTTOM Give me your neaf, Mounsieur Mustardseed. Pray you, leave your courtesy, good Mounsieur.

MUSTARDSEED What's your will?

BOTTOM Nothing, good Mounsieur, but to help Cavalery Peaseblossom to scratch. I must to the barber's, Mounsieur, for methinks I am marvellous hairy about the face. And I am such a tender ass, if my hair do but tickle me, I must scratch.

TITANIA What, wilt thou hear some music, my sweet love?

BOTTOM I have a reasonable good ear in music. Let's have the tongs and the bones.

TITANIA Or say, sweet love, what thou desir'st to eat.

BOTTOM Truly, a peck of provender, I could munch your good dry oats. Methinks I have a great desire to a bottle of hay. Good hay, sweet hay hath no fellow.

Bottom and Titania sleep. Oberon talks to Puck about his pity for Titania, and how she has returned the changeling boy. He removes the spell from her.

Language in the play

'O, how I love thee! How I dote on thee!'

a How do you respond to Titania's language in the script opposite? Decide what you think this scene reveals about her character and consider how an audience might react to her words. Describe this reaction in one word.

b Oberon says about Titania, 'Her dotage now I do begin to pity' (line 44). Do you think his words cause a change in the audience's feeling towards Titania at this point in the play? What single word would you choose now to describe the audience's reaction?

Write about it

Titania and Bottom

a The picture below is powerful and amusing, but also rather disturbing. What type of relationship is being presented in this production? Compare it to the image on page 100. Consider the effects of the two pictures on a live audience. What aspects of each character and their situations are emphasised in each image?

b Write for ten minutes, analysing the detail in these two photographs. Begin with costume and staging.

venturous audacious, risk-taking

exposition of (another of Bottom's mistakes; he means he is disposed to sleep)

wind thee in my arms put my arms around you

be all ways away be off in every direction

dotage foolishness, infatuation

upbraid tell off, scold

orient lustrous, eastern

bewail lament, grieve over

swain lover

repair return

fierce vexation unpleasant aggravation

TITANIA I have a venturous fairy that shall seek
The squirrel's hoard, and fetch thee new nuts.

BOTTOM I had rather have a handful or two of dried peas. But, I pray you, let none of your people stir me; I have an exposition of sleep come upon me.

TITANIA Sleep thou, and I will wind thee in my arms.
Fairies be gone, and be all ways away.

[*Exeunt Fairies*]

So doth the woodbine the sweet honeysuckle
Gently entwist; the female ivy so
Enrings the barky fingers of the elm.
O, how I love thee! How I dote on thee!

[*They sleep.*]

Enter PUCK.

OBERON [*Coming forward.*]
Welcome, good Robin. Seest thou this sweet sight?
Her dotage now I do begin to pity;
For, meeting her of late behind the wood
Seeking sweet favours for this hateful fool,
I did upbraid her and fall out with her,
For she his hairy temples then had rounded
With coronet of fresh and fragrant flowers;
And that same dew, which sometime on the buds
Was wont to swell like round and orient pearls,
Stood now within the pretty flowerets' eyes
Like tears that did their own disgrace bewail.
When I had at my pleasure taunted her,
And she in mild terms begged my patience,
I then did ask of her her changeling child,
Which straight she gave me, and her fairy sent
To bear him to my bower in Fairyland.
And now I have the boy, I will undo
This hateful imperfection of her eyes.
And, gentle Puck, take this transformèd scalp
From off the head of this Athenian swain,
That, he awaking when the other do,
May all to Athens back again repair,
And think no more of this night's accidents
But as the fierce vexation of a dream.
But first I will release the Fairy Queen.

[*Squeezing a herb on Titania's eyes.*]

Titania wakes, and she and Oberon are reconciled. Puck removes the ass's head from Bottom. All leave except the 'mortals' (the lovers and Bottom).

1 Music and dance = harmony (in pairs)

The resolution of the conflict between Titania and Oberon is marked by both dance and music. In Elizabethan times, the harmony of music was often taken as a symbol of human harmony. The music and dance in modern productions vary widely. Sometimes they are formal and dignified, sometimes wildly extravagant.

What kind of music and dance do you think is suitable for this moment in the play? Develop a short dance for Titania and Oberon, perhaps to some appropriate music you have found or have created yourselves.

Themes

Gender and power

Up to this point in the play, Oberon's language has been consistently assertive. But between lines 82 and 95 in the script opposite, it is markedly different in style and tone from his first speeches in Act 2 Scene 1 (lines 60–80). There, his diction and syntax are commanding ('Am I not thy lord?', line 63). However, there are still elements of this attempted dominance here: 'Titania, music call'. His language is abrupt and he clearly still expects to be obeyed.

Make a list of the similarities and differences in Oberon's language here compared with his earlier appearances, and suggest possible reasons for this change. Remember, the quarrel is resolved and he and Titania are now in harmony; however, Oberon is very much in control and has achieved his aims.

wast wont used, was accustomed

Dian's bud (possibly the antidote to Cupid's flower)

Methought I thought

enamoured of infatuated, besotted with

strike more … common sleep Oberon asks for silence and gentle music so that the lovers and Bottom do not wake

amity friendly relations

fair prosperity as promised

mark notice

compass go round

Be as thou wast wont to be;
See as thou wast wont to see.
Dian's bud o'er Cupid's flower
Hath such force and blessèd power.
Now, my Titania, wake you, my sweet Queen!

TITANIA [*Starting up.*]
My Oberon, what visions have I seen!
Methought I was enamoured of an ass.

OBERON There lies your love.

TITANIA How came these things to pass?
O, how mine eyes do loathe his visage now!

OBERON Silence awhile: Robin, take off this head.
Titania, music call, and strike more dead
Than common sleep of all these five the sense.

TITANIA Music, ho, music such as charmeth sleep!
[*Soft music plays.*]

PUCK [*To Bottom, removing the ass's head*]
Now when thou wak'st, with thine own fool's eyes peep.

OBERON Sound, music! Come, my Queen, take hands with me,
And rock the ground whereon these sleepers be.
[*They dance.*]
Now thou and I are new in amity,
And will tomorrow midnight solemnly
Dance in Duke Theseus' house triumphantly,
And bless it to all fair prosperity.
There shall the pairs of faithful lovers be
Wedded, with Theseus, all in jollity.

PUCK Fairy King, attend, and mark:
I do hear the morning lark.

OBERON Then, my Queen, in silence sad,
Trip we after night's shade;
We the globe can compass soon,
Swifter than the wandering moon.

TITANIA Come, my lord, and in our flight
Tell me how it came this night
That I sleeping here was found
With these mortals on the ground.
Exeunt Oberon, Titania and Puck

Theseus, Hippolyta and the others enter, on an early morning hunting expedition. After praising the barking of the hounds, they find the sleeping lovers.

Write about it

From night to day

The transition between the exit of the fairies at line 99 and the entrance of the court moves the action from the fairy world of moonlight to the daylight world of the mortals.

Write a paragraph describing how you would signal this change on stage in a dramatically effective way.

Stagecraft

In praise of hunting dogs (in pairs)

a Theseus's and Hippolyta's speeches about the hounds may be difficult for a modern audience to understand. Take parts and speak lines 100–23, then discuss how you think the lines could be delivered on stage to engage the imagination and interest of the audience.

b Would you cut some of these lines for a modern production? What argument would you use to convince a director to cut or to keep? Record your ideas in your Director's Journal.

1 Theseus – a joke? And a warning? (in pairs)

a 'The rite of May' (line 130) connects with the festivals of Elizabethan England (as does the title of the play itself). In some of these festivals, ordinary behaviour and laws were dispensed with. Such festivals celebrated disorder and allowed people to behave in a way that was free of ordinary constraints. In performance, Theseus's words 'No doubt they rose up early to observe / The rite of May' (lines 129–30) often provoke audience laughter. Talk together about whether you think that is an appropriate response – and why.

b In lines 132–3, Theseus says:

But speak, Egeus; is this not the day
That Hermia should give the answer of her choice?

Is this a menacing moment? Remember the threat to put Hermia in a convent or execute her. Consider how Theseus might speak these lines. How might the lovers react to both? Make suggestions for all the actors.

observation is performed Mayday festivities are completed

vaward early part

Uncouple unleash them

Dispatch send them off

Cadmus mythical founder of Thebes

bayed the bear tamed the bear with their barking

Crete … Sparta both famous for their hunting hounds

chiding yelping

So flewed, so sanded with similar jowls and similar sandy colouring

dewlapped with loose neck skin

matched in mouth like bells loud as bells

tuneable melodious

hallooed called, shouted

Thessaly region of Greece

rite of May festival in May to give thanks for a good spring harvest

in grace of our solemnity in honour of our marriage

Wind horns. Enter THESEUS *with* HIPPOLYTA, EGEUS, *and all his train.*

THESEUS Go, one of you, find out the forester;
For now our observation is performed,
And since we have the vaward of the day,
My love shall hear the music of my hounds.
Uncouple in the western valley; let them go:
Dispatch, I say, and find the forester.

[*Exit an Attendant*]

We will, fair Queen, up to the mountain's top,
And mark the musical confusion
Of hounds and echo in conjunction.

HIPPOLYTA I was with Hercules and Cadmus once,
When in a wood of Crete they bayed the bear
With hounds of Sparta: never did I hear
Such gallant chiding; for besides the groves,
The skies, the fountains, every region near
Seemed all one mutual cry. I never heard
So musical a discord, such sweet thunder.

THESEUS My hounds are bred out of the Spartan kind,
So flewed, so sanded; and their heads are hung
With ears that sweep away the morning dew;
Crook-kneed, and dewlapped like Thessalian bulls;
Slow in pursuit, but matched in mouth like bells,
Each under each. A cry more tuneable
Was never hallooed to nor cheered with horn
In Crete, in Sparta, nor in Thessaly.
Judge when you hear. But soft, what nymphs are these?

EGEUS My lord, this is my daughter here asleep,
And this Lysander; this Demetrius is,
This Helena, old Nedar's Helena.
I wonder of their being here together.

THESEUS No doubt they rose up early to observe
The rite of May, and hearing our intent
Came here in grace of our solemnity.
But speak, Egeus; is not this the day
That Hermia should give answer of her choice?

EGEUS It is, my lord.

The lovers are woken by shouts and blasts on horns. Lysander tries to explain what has happened. Egeus urges Theseus to punish Lysander for attempting to elope with Hermia.

1 The dance of the lovers – who loves whom? (IV)

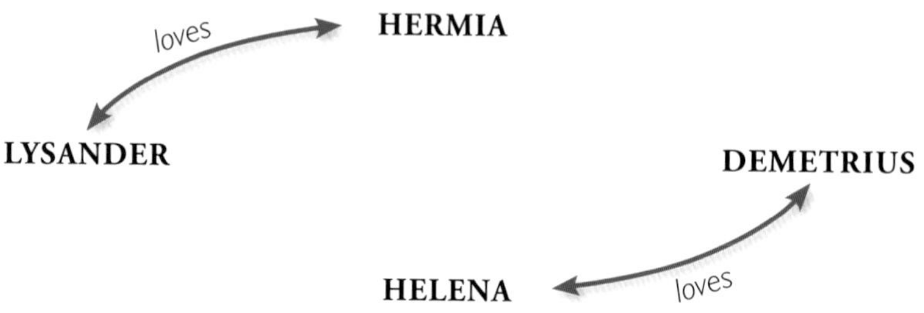

This is the final arrangement of the lovers. Look back at how the 'dance' of the lovers has progressed through the play, on pages 10, 50 and 76. Compare all the dances and identify what patterns emerge.

Stagecraft

Just how do they awake? **(in small groups)**

The lovers '*all start up*'. But how? Puck has ensured that when each awakes they will first see the person they love. Put the stage direction into action by performing their awakening. Remember, each character first sees his or her lover, then Theseus and his court – with Egeus.

Characters

Egeus – still an angry father

Egeus, having not experienced the night's 'dreams', persists in viewing the world as one in conflict. He continues to demand his legal rights as an Athenian father. For him, the 'dream' has had no effect on the real world.

This is the last time Egeus speaks in the play. What are your final thoughts on him? Write a brief character sketch as a guide for an actor preparing to play this part.

Saint Valentine (a popular belief was that birds chose their mates on St Valentine's Day)

couple pair up

concord harmony

jealousy mistrust

enmity hostility

amazedly in an amazed manner

bethink me remember

our intent our intention, plan

Without the peril beyond the danger

defeated cheated

THESEUS Go, bid the huntsmen wake them with their horns.
Shout within; wind horns; [*the lovers*] *all start up.*
Good morrow, friends. Saint Valentine is past;
Begin these woodbirds but to couple now?
[*The lovers kneel.*]
LYSANDER Pardon, my lord.
THESEUS I pray you all, stand up.
I know you two are rival enemies:
How comes this gentle concord in the world,
That hatred is so far from jealousy
To sleep by hate, and fear no enmity?
LYSANDER My lord, I shall reply amazedly,
Half sleep, half waking; but as yet, I swear,
I cannot truly say how I came here.
But as I think (for truly would I speak)
And now I do bethink me, so it is –
I came with Hermia hither. Our intent
Was to be gone from Athens, where we might
Without the peril of the Athenian law –
EGEUS Enough, enough, my lord; you have enough –
I beg the law, the law upon his head!
They would have stol'n away, they would, Demetrius,
Thereby to have defeated you and me,
You of your wife, and me of my consent,
Of my consent that she should be your wife.

Demetrius explains his love for Hermia has melted and he loves Helena, now and evermore. Theseus instructs the lovers to come with him to be married. All leave except the lovers.

Language in the play

Romantic and heartfelt

a Demetrius's lines 172–3 are very emotional:

Now I do wish it, love it, long for it,
And will for evermore be true to it.

Will speeches such as this make all Helena's suffering and humiliation worthwhile for her? Write a paragraph in the form of a diary entry, describing how she feels on hearing these words.

b Demetrius's speech is a heartfelt exploration of the nature of love. He uses evocative imagery – toys and trinkets, sickness and health and taste and food – to describe his feelings. Analyse the language of love in Demetrius's speech and then write a paragraph responding to this question: 'How does Shakespeare present love through Demetrius's language?'

c Theseus made a joke about St Valentine's Day at line 136. *A Midsummer Night's Dream* is a romantic comedy full of beautiful verse. Which lines in the play would make appropriate verses for a Valentine's Day card? Design your card with a dream theme, using a quotation from the play.

Themes

Dominant men? (in small groups)

At this moment, Theseus is the dominant character.

a In your group, take turns to read aloud all Theseus's speeches in Scene 1, then speak Oberon's lines from earlier in the scene. Talk together about the similarities and differences between the two characters, list your ideas and then use them to create a Venn diagram like the one below.

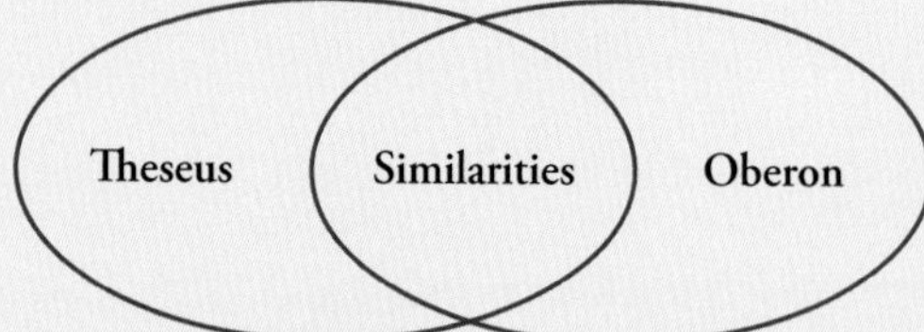

b Discuss these statements:

- Both the fairy and mortal worlds are totally dominated by men.
- Shakespeare presents clear limitations to male power in this play.

stealth secrecy

in fancy doting, in love

idle gaud worthless toy

discourse conversation

overbear your will overrule your wishes

eternally be knit be bound together forever

something worn somewhat spent, nearly over

solemnity celebration

DEMETRIUS My lord, fair Helen told me of their stealth,
Of this their purpose hither to this wood;
And I in fury hither followed them,
Fair Helena in fancy following me.
But, my good lord, I wot not by what power
(But by some power it is), my love to Hermia,
Melted as the snow, seems to me now
As the remembrance of an idle gaud
Which in my childhood I did dote upon;
And all the faith, the virtue of my heart,
The object and the pleasure of mine eye,
Is only Helena. To her, my lord,
Was I betrothed ere I saw Hermia;
But like a sickness did I loathe this food.
But, as in health come to my natural taste,
Now I do wish it, love it, long for it,
And will for evermore be true to it.

THESEUS Fair lovers, you are fortunately met.
Of this discourse we more will hear anon.
Egeus, I will overbear your will;
For in the temple, by and by, with us
These couples shall eternally be knit.
And, for the morning now is something worn,
Our purposed hunting shall be set aside.
Away with us to Athens. Three and three,
We'll hold a feast in great solemnity.
Come, Hippolyta.

Exit Theseus with Hippolyta, Egeus, and his train

The lovers wonder if they are dreaming, agree they are awake, and follow the duke. Bottom wakes, and wonders at his 'dream'.

1 Reflections on dreaming – the lovers (in fours)

a Take the parts of the lovers, and read aloud their short moment of reflection here (lines 184–96). Then talk together about the different ways in which the lovers describe their experiences. Consider each speech in turn and suggest how it could be delivered on stage.

b Demetrius says 'let us recount our dreams' as they walk back to Athens. In role, do just that. Each character tells not only what they think happened, but also what they have learned about their behaviour, their relationships and about love.

Language in the play

Similes and metaphors

Each of the four lovers tries to describe their thoughts using a variety of similes and metaphors. Pick the one you like the most and analyse it in as much detail as you can.

2 Reflections on dreaming – Bottom (in pairs)

a Individually, read and make notes on Bottom's reflections, which he speaks alone on stage.

b Identify the lines in Bottom's speech that have similarities with this passage in the Bible:

> *But as it is written, Eye hath not seen, nor ear heard, neither have entered into the heart of man, the things which God hath prepared for them that love him.*
>
> I Corinthians 2.9

Speculate on the purpose of this connection.

c Bottom says he will get Peter Quince to write a ballad called 'Bottom's Dream'. Write and perform your own version of the ballad.

Write about it

Bottom the philosopher

Bottom appears to be at his most philosophical here. What might he have learned about love, life and himself? Choose the most revealing words and phrases to describe his experience. Write about 100 words on how the events of the previous night have changed his character. Use your chosen quotations to support your ideas.

undistinguishable indiscernible, barely visible

parted eye unfocused, seeing double

patched fool a Fool (who wore a traditional patchwork costume)

ballad simple song

hath no bottom is profound and deep

Peradventure perhaps

gracious appealing

her death (referring to Thisbe in the Mechanicals' play)

DEMETRIUS These things seem small and undistinguishable,
Like far-off mountains turnèd into clouds.

HERMIA Methinks I see these things with parted eye,
When everything seems double.

HELENA So methinks;
And I have found Demetrius, like a jewel,
Mine own, and not mine own.

DEMETRIUS Are you sure
That we are awake? It seems to me
That yet we sleep, we dream. Do not you think
The Duke was here, and bid us follow him?

HERMIA Yea, and my father.

HELENA And Hippolyta.

LYSANDER And he did bid us follow to the temple.

DEMETRIUS Why, then, we are awake. Let's follow him,
And by the way let us recount our dreams.

Exeunt lovers

Bottom wakes.

BOTTOM When my cue comes, call me, and I will answer. My next is 'Most fair Pyramus'. Heigh ho! Peter Quince? Flute the bellows-mender? Snout the tinker? Starveling? God's my life! Stolen hence and left me asleep! I have had a most rare vision. I have had a dream, past the wit of man to say what dream it was. Man is but an ass if he go about to expound this dream. Methought I was – there is no man can tell what. Methought I was – and methought I had – but man is but a patched fool if he will offer to say what methought I had. The eye of man hath not heard, the ear of man hath not seen, man's hand is not able to taste, his tongue to conceive, nor his heart to report what my dream was! I will get Peter Quince to write a ballad of this dream; it shall be called 'Bottom's Dream', because it hath no bottom; and I will sing it in the latter end of a play, before the Duke. Peradventure, to make it the more gracious, I shall sing it at her death. *Exit*

The Mechanicals, without Bottom, despair (they had been looking forward to a regular salary from the duke for their performance). But Bottom suddenly arrives with the news that their play has been chosen.

1 The Mechanicals: a team? (in fives)

Throughout the play, the audience has been witness to formal justice, magic, love, conflict – and here we have a moment of real friendship.

a Take parts and read the whole scene opposite.

b Talk together about what sort of relationship the Mechanicals seem to have at this moment. Consider, in particular, how the group feels about Bottom. Where would you find evidence in the rest of the play for your conclusions?

c Compare your impression with the picture below and with the images on pages 18, 22 and 56.

2 Prediction

The audience now knows that the Mechanicals are to perform their play for Duke Theseus, and has already seen them in rehearsal. Make some predictions on how you think the performance will go. Consider in detail each character, the part they are to play and the impression of the whole performance so far.

Out of doubt there is no doubt

transported carried away

marred spoiled

discharge perform

handicraft man skilled craftsman

A paramour … thing of naught a mistress and, to Flute, something immoral and wicked; Quince meant 'paragon', a model of excellence

we had all been made men our fortunes would be made (they will be paid sixpence a day if they perform)

sweet bully Bottom dear, fine Bottom

hearts friends, dear ones

courageous day fine/splendid day

good strings to your beards strong strings to tie on your false beards

pumps shoes

presently immediately

preferred recommended for performance

linen underclothes

Act 4 Scene 2
Athens

Enter QUINCE, FLUTE, SNOUT *and* STARVELING.

QUINCE Have you sent to Bottom's house? Is he come home yet?

STARVELING He cannot be heard of. Out of doubt he is transported.

FLUTE If he come not, then the play is marred. It goes not forward. Doth it?

QUINCE It is not possible. You have not a man in all Athens able to discharge Pyramus but he.

FLUTE No, he hath simply the best wit of any handicraft man in Athens.

QUINCE Yea, and the best person, too; and he is a very paramour for a sweet voice.

FLUTE You must say 'paragon'. A paramour is (God bless us!) a thing of naught. *Enter* SNUG *the joiner.*

SNUG Masters, the Duke is coming from the temple, and there is two or three lords and ladies more married. If our sport had gone forward, we had all been made men.

FLUTE O, sweet bully Bottom! Thus hath he lost sixpence a day during his life: he could not have 'scaped sixpence a day. And the Duke had not given him sixpence a day for playing Pyramus, I'll be hanged. He would have deserved it. Sixpence a day in Pyramus, or nothing. *Enter* BOTTOM.

BOTTOM Where are these lads? Where are these hearts?

QUINCE Bottom! O most courageous day! O most happy hour!

BOTTOM Masters, I am to discourse wonders – but ask me not what; for if I tell you, I am not true Athenian. I will tell you everything, right as it fell out.

QUINCE Let us hear, sweet Bottom.

BOTTOM Not a word of me. All that I will tell you is – that the Duke hath dined. Get your apparel together, good strings to your beards, new ribbons to your pumps: meet presently at the palace, every man look o'er his part. For the short and the long is, our play is preferred. In any case, let Thisbe have clean linen; and let not him that plays the lion pare his nails, for they shall hang out for the lion's claws. And, most dear actors, eat no onions nor garlic; for we are to utter sweet breath, and I do not doubt but to hear them say it is a sweet comedy. No more words. Away! Go, away! *Exeunt*

Looking back at Act 4

Activities for groups or individuals

1 All conflict ended

In most plays, conflicts are not resolved until the final scene. But *A Midsummer Night's Dream* is different. Only Egeus remains unsatisfied, and he does not appear again. The play's conflicts are ended, but there is still one more act to come. This is a good moment to list the conflicts that the play has explored. Write them down and then consider:

- the themes and ideas that Shakespeare explores though each conflict
- the language used to describe each theme/idea (you may want to refer back to the binary oppositions explored on page 98 and consider submission versus defiance, duty versus honour and dreams versus reality)
- how each conflict is resolved.

Now write a paragraph in which you analyse each point of conflict. Justify your ideas with evidence from the text.

2 Titania and Hippolyta: power and context

You could think of both Titania and Hippolyta as 'vanquished' women who have to learn their 'duty' to their lord. But many productions use all types of stage business to show that these characters are not without power and influence.

a Remind yourself of all Titania's and Hippolyta's appearances in the play so far. Then write notes on how the language Shakespeare gives them, and the non-verbal techniques an actor can use, show them to have independence of spirit and action.

▼ Titania and Oberon's conflict comes to an end, and the couple dance together.

b What aspects of Titania and Hippolyta's behaviour might a twenty-first-century audience find difficult to understand or sympathise with? If you could alter the script, what changes to the lines of these two characters would you suggest?

c What ideas do you have for how Hippolyta and Titania should be played? Write suggestions for the director of a modern production of the play.

d Discuss as a group the similarities and differences in the issues that the female characters in the play face with those that women face in the twenty-first century.

3 Exploring Shakespeare's imagination

Shakespeare has presented a complex 'dream world' that raises many questions. Here are some to start you thinking:

- What does each group of characters believe about this dream world?
- What do you make of it?
- Whose imagination is at work here: the characters', Shakespeare's, the audience's?

In groups of three, each take responsibility for one of the following:

- Bottom
- Titania
- the lovers.

Research, reflect and make notes on their particular experiences or dreams, how the 'dreams' were presented to the audience, how the experience was described, and the consequences of and changes wrought by the experience.

In turn, share your ideas. Then together discuss the play in relation to imagination, individual psychology and the worlds of dream and reality.

4 Celebrity stories

Complete one of the following tasks:

a Today, gossip columns and celebrity magazines would be having a field day with the prospect of so many high-profile weddings to come. Write two or three magazine or newspaper gossip stories based on the events of the play up to the end of Act 4. What sort of background details would journalists be interested in? Who would they want to quote? Have they found out about the strange night in the woods?

b Compose a tabloid newspaper or gossip magazine 'scoop' on the upcoming weddings. Speculate on the scandal, headlines, expense, dress designers and so on. Think carefully about your writing style and target audience.

5 Fairies – an assignment

An actor who played a fairy in *A Midsummer Night's Dream* once said, 'The minute you say "fairy" to people, they think they know exactly what it is.' People have preconceived ideas about what fairies look like and how they behave. Modern audiences may well perceive fairies as comical, whereas the Elizabethans' belief in the supernatural may have made for a more serious approach.

Prepare an assignment on fairies. It can include notes, different types of illustrations, extracts from the play and so on. To get started, look at the many images of fairies in this edition. Also consider the fairies' names, and what they do in the play. Then reflect on these possibilities:

- non-human spirits and their capacity for good and evil
- fairies at the bottom of the garden
- the fairies' function of bringing on stage the world of fantasy and imagination
- fairies as representatives of magical and spiritual forces in human lives.

You may also want to read 'Fairies and magic', page 153.

6 A fifty-word summary

Write an account of what happens in Act 4 in exactly fifty words.

Theseus and Hippolyta talk about the lovers' story, and the power of imagination in poet, lover and madman – who all see things that are not there.

Stagecraft

Return to Athens (in pairs)

In Act 5, Shakespeare returns the action to Theseus's palace in Athens. As set designers, you and a partner need to decide if the set should remain identical to the one at the start of the play, or if you should focus on revealing parallels, echoes and developments that have taken place. Think about what has happened in the time since the audience last saw Athens. Draw up a proposal for the director to consider.

Write about it

Shakespeare's poetry (in pairs)

Shakespeare was a poet as well as a playwright. The speeches of Theseus (and also those of Titania) are considered to be among the finest examples of Shakespeare's dramatic poetry. Sometimes actors playing Theseus are criticised for speaking the lines opposite simply as poetry, rather than as part of the dramatic script of a play.

a Talk together about what you consider to be the differences between 'poetry' and 'dramatic poetry'. Pool your ideas on how the actors could deliver the lines to ensure that the audience experiences both 'poetry' and 'drama'. Put your ideas into practice by performing the lines.

b It is interesting that Theseus does not believe the lovers' story. Analyse his speech (lines 2–22) in detail. He begins sceptically and then explores the power of the imagination, which creates madmen but also inspires the poet.

c On your own, write a paragraph in which you respond to the ideas that Theseus expresses in the script opposite. Do you think his views on literature have any relevance to this play?

antique ancient, grotesque or absurd

toys tales

seething agitated

lunatic madness brought about by changes in the moon

compact composed

Helen Helen of Troy (a legendary beauty)

bodies forth embodies in a way that the mind can take in

tricks self-deception

transfigured changed into something beautiful

constancy certainty

admirable marvellous

Act 5 Scene 1
Athens Theseus' palace

Enter THESEUS, HIPPOLYTA, PHILOSTRATE, *Lords and Attendants.*

HIPPOLYTA 'Tis strange, my Theseus, that these lovers speak of.
THESEUS More strange than true. I never may believe
These antique fables, nor these fairy toys.
Lovers and madmen have such seething brains,
Such shaping fantasies, that apprehend
More than cool reason ever comprehends.
The lunatic, the lover, and the poet
Are of imagination all compact:
One sees more devils than vast hell can hold;
That is the madman. The lover, all as frantic,
Sees Helen's beauty in a brow of Egypt.
The poet's eye, in a fine frenzy rolling,
Doth glance from heaven to earth, from earth to heaven;
And as imagination bodies forth
The forms of things unknown, the poet's pen
Turns them to shapes, and gives to airy nothing
A local habitation and a name.
Such tricks hath strong imagination
That if it would but apprehend some joy,
It comprehends some bringer of that joy;
Or in the night, imagining some fear,
How easy is a bush supposed a bear?
HIPPOLYTA But all the story of the night told over,
And all their minds transfigured so together,
More witnesseth than fancy's images,
And grows to something of great constancy;
But howsoever, strange and admirable.

The lovers enter, and Theseus looks through the list of performances ready for the evening's entertainment. He rejects the first three, but is attracted by the play *Pyramus and Thisbe*.

Stagecraft

Staging the play within a play

Look carefully at the photograph below, which shows how this important scene was set in a recent production. Make a list of the decisions that have been made about the set and the positioning of the actors. Consider the practical and dramatic implications of those decisions. Suggest three improvements you would make.

board … bed board and lodging

masques dances or entertainments where masks were worn

after-supper dessert

manager of mirth organiser and selector of entertainment (Philostrate performs this role for Theseus; in a similar way, Elizabeth I's Master of Entertainment, Sir Edward Tilney, selected the best plays for her)

abridgement entertainment for making time go quickly, pastime

beguile cheat

brief summary

ripe ready

eunuch castrated man

tipsy Bacchanals drunken women (from Greek mythology)

Thracian from Greece

device entertainment

Muses goddesses of learning and art

Of learning … in beggary (poets and scholars traditionally die in poverty)

satire keen sharp ridicule

Not sorting with not appropriate to

tragical mirth an oxymoron (like 'hot ice'): the Mechanicals' play can't be both tragic and funny

concord harmony

Enter the lovers: LYSANDER, DEMETRIUS, HERMIA *and* HELENA.

THESEUS Here come the lovers, full of joy and mirth.
Joy, gentle friends, joy and fresh days of love
Accompany your hearts!

LYSANDER More than to us
Wait in your royal walks, your board, your bed!

THESEUS Come now: what masques, what dances shall we have
To wear away this long age of three hours
Between our after-supper and bedtime?
Where is our usual manager of mirth?
What revels are in hand? Is there no play
To ease the anguish of a torturing hour?
Call Philostrate.

PHILOSTRATE Here, mighty Theseus.

THESEUS Say, what abridgement have you for this evening?
What masque, what music? How shall we beguile
The lazy time if not with some delight?

PHILOSTRATE [*Giving him a paper.*]
There is a brief how many sports are ripe.
Make choice of which your highness will see first.

THESEUS [*Reading.*]
'The battle with the Centaurs, to be sung
By an Athenian eunuch to the harp' –
We'll none of that; that have I told my love
In glory of my kinsman, Hercules.
[*Reading.*] 'The riot of the tipsy Bacchanals,
Tearing the Thracian singer in their rage' –
That is an old device, and it was played
When I from Thebes came last a conqueror.
[*Reading.*] 'The thrice three Muses mourning for the death
Of learning, late deceased in beggary' –
That is some satire keen and critical,
Not sorting with a nuptial ceremony.
[*Reading.*] 'A tedious brief scene of young Pyramus
And his love Thisbe, very tragical mirth' –
Merry and tragical? Tedious and brief?
That is hot ice and wondrous strange snow!
How shall we find the concord of this discord?

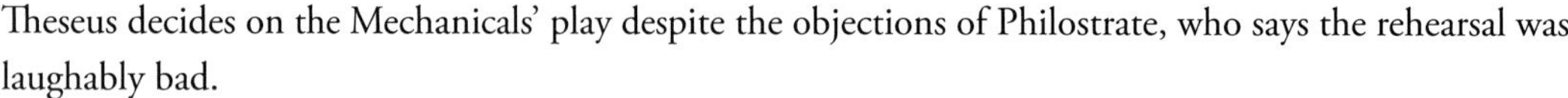

Theseus decides on the Mechanicals' play despite the objections of Philostrate, who says the rehearsal was laughably bad.

1 Philostrate – a snob? (in pairs)

Philostrate picks out the key words from the Mechanicals' description of their play and uses these words to convince Theseus that the play is not worth seeing. Take turns to catch his superior tone of voice. Afterwards, discuss whether he is being fair to the Mechanicals. Do you think he might be concerned as much with their social class as by the quality of their performance?

Stagecraft

Two audiences – two responses (in pairs)

The Mechanicals will perform to two audiences: the court characters on stage, and the real theatre audience. So the theatre audience is able to witness the characters' responses to the Mechanicals' play as well as watching the play itself. This is quite demanding on the audience, as it demands focus on two areas of the stage at once, but it also allows more opportunity for humour: the play and the response. The theatre audience also gets an outsider's view of the Mechanicals' play through Philostrate's description.

a Suggest reasons why Shakespeare included Philostrate's description of the play (after all, both audiences are about to see it). Discuss whether you think that both audiences will react in the same way (you will soon discover the views of the onstage audience).

b Think of other plays, movies and books that 'layer' your responses (that is, you respond to the performance and to the onstage audience's response). Examples are *Hamlet*, the movie *The Truman Show* and 'The Tale of the Three Brothers' in *Harry Potter and the Deathly Hallows*. Discuss the dramatic effect of such layering.

Characters

Hippolyta's response: 'I love not to see …'

Like Philostrate, Hippolyta is also worried about seeing the performance, but her motivation appears to be different.

a Summarise her argument in a couple of sentences.

b How might Hippolyta speak lines 85–6? Suggest what they reveal about her. As you read on, compare her words to the men's responses.

apt appropriate

'merry' tears crying with laughter

Hard-handed men men who work with their hands

toiled worked until weary

unbreathed unpractised

sport fun, entertainment

Extremely stretched stretched beyond their limits

conned learnt

simpleness artless and natural sincerity

tender it offer it

wretchedness o'ercharged those of little ability overstretched (or poor people mocked)

perishing not surviving the experience

PHILOSTRATE A play there is, my lord, some ten words long,
Which is as 'brief' as I have known a play,
But by ten words, my lord, it is too long,
Which makes it 'tedious'. For in all the play
There is not one word apt, one player fitted.
And 'tragical', my noble lord, it is,
For Pyramus therein doth kill himself,
Which when I saw rehearsed, I must confess,
Made mine eyes water; but more 'merry' tears
The passion of loud laughter never shed.

THESEUS What are they that do play it?

PHILOSTRATE Hard-handed men that work in Athens here,
Which never laboured in their minds till now;
And now have toiled their unbreathed memories
With this same play against your nuptial.

THESEUS And we will hear it.

PHILOSTRATE No, my noble lord,
It is not for you. I have heard it over,
And it is nothing, nothing in the world,
Unless you can find sport in their intents,
Extremely stretched, and conned with cruel pain,
To do you service.

THESEUS I will hear that play;
For never anything can be amiss
When simpleness and duty tender it.
Go bring them in; and take your places, ladies.
[*Exit Philostrate*]

HIPPOLYTA I love not to see wretchedness o'ercharged,
And duty in his service perishing.

THESEUS Why, gentle sweet, you shall see no such thing.

HIPPOLYTA He says they can do nothing in this kind.

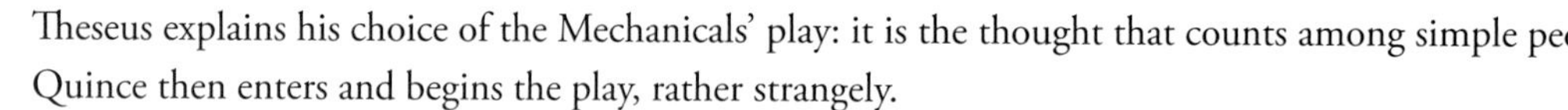
Theseus explains his choice of the Mechanicals' play: it is the thought that counts among simple people. Quince then enters and begins the play, rather strangely.

1 On show – does it make you tongue-tied? (in pairs)

We are all on show to others every time we are in public. But great occasions can stop us speaking altogether. In lines 93–105, Theseus talks about learned people such as 'great clerks' being unable to talk during official welcomes. He also criticises the 'audacious eloquence', or insincerity, of those who speak a little too well in public. Theseus prefers 'love' (in the sense of sincere affection) and 'tongue-tied simplicity': those who speak little ('least') communicate a great deal ('speak most'). Theseus feels that it is important to understand the speaker's intentions even when the language and delivery is mismanaged and poorly performed.

With a partner, talk about the prospect of speaking in public. What are the three elements that would help ensure a confident and successful speech? Make notes and then compare your ideas with another pair.

Language in the play

Watch your punctuation! (in pairs)

Quince's Prologue (lines 108–17) has much of its punctuation in the wrong place (that's why the court jokes about his 'points' and 'stops' – the punctuation).

a One person delivers his speech as it is written. The other improves the punctuation to make better sense, and then reads this version. Which one works best dramatically? Why?

b Look at the word choices and repetitions in the Prologue, and together come up with one observation on what it reveals about Quince. Share this with the class.

Stagecraft

Asides: does Quince hear? (in fours)

a Discuss whether Quince hears the comments of the court (lines 118–23), or whether they are **asides** (heard only by the audience).

b Try acting it out both ways: if Quince hears, he will react; if he doesn't, he simply carries on. Remember, 'dramatic effect' is your guide: what the audience most enjoys.

Keep this 'overhearing' notion in mind for the rest of the Mechanicals' play.

in might, not merit accepts it, given the ability of those that offer it

clerks men of learning

purposèd approached

premeditated welcomes planned speeches

periods stops

midst middle

Throttle choke on

dumbly silenced

rattling tongue talking too much

saucy flippant, cheeky

audacious eloquence daring communication

capacity understanding

addressed ready

in despite to be annoying and troublesome

stand upon points take notice of punctuation or detail (Quince's misuse of punctuation makes his prologue confusing and ambiguous)

rough colt untamed young horse

stop a pun on full stop, and suddenly stopping a horse when riding

in government under control

THESEUS The kinder we, to give them thanks for nothing.
Our sport shall be to take what they mistake;
And what poor duty cannot do, noble respect
Takes it in might, not merit.
Where I have come, great clerks have purposèd
To greet me with premeditated welcomes,
Where I have seen them shiver and look pale,
Make periods in the midst of sentences,
Throttle their practised accent in their fears,
And in conclusion dumbly have broke off,
Not paying me a welcome. Trust me, sweet,
Out of this silence yet I picked a welcome,
And in the modesty of fearful duty
I read as much as from the rattling tongue
Of saucy and audacious eloquence.
Love, therefore, and tongue-tied simplicity
In least speak most, to my capacity.

[*Enter Philostrate.*]

PHILOSTRATE So please your grace, the Prologue is addressed.
THESEUS Let him approach.

Flourish of trumpets.

Enter QUINCE *as Prologue.*

QUINCE If we offend, it is with our good will.
That you should think, we come not to offend,
But with good will. To show our simple skill,
That is the true beginning of our end.
Consider then, we come but in despite.
We do not come as minding to content you,
Our true intent is. All for your delight,
We are not here. That you should here repent you,
The actors are at hand; and by their show
You shall know all that you are like to know.

THESEUS This fellow doth not stand upon points.

LYSANDER He hath rid his prologue like a rough colt; he knows not the stop. A good moral, my lord; it is not enough to speak, but to speak true.

HIPPOLYTA Indeed, he hath played on this prologue like a child on a recorder – a sound, but not in government.

Theseus comments on how mixed up Quince's introduction was. Quince continues with the Prologue, which explains the play, and introduces the characters.

1 The Prologue – an outline of the play (in sixes)

Quince's description of the play the Mechanicals are about to perform usually generates a lot of laughter among the audience in the theatre. This is your chance to work on the lines to create a very funny performance. Take parts and work on the following activities.

a Entrances and exits At the beginning of the Prologue, all the Mechanicals come on to the stage and all but Snout exit at the end of it. How would you have them do this? For example, it might be a noisy and messy entrance and exit, with the Mechanicals nervous and excited; or perhaps more subdued – overawed by the occasion. Try out a few different ideas.

b Mime to the Prologue As Quince speaks the Prologue, each of the Mechanicals comes forward to mime the character or object they are portraying. Experiment with different ways of presenting your mimes. You may want to act over the top, or stumbling and muddling, or in any other way that you think might work. Is it possible to be funny, foolish and endearing at once? It is important that the audience laughs but also empathises. Try out ways to achieve that response.

c The play itself Talk together about what the Prologue suggests about the sort of play the Mechanicals will present. Also discuss the likely dramatic impact of such a description, and what this tells you about the Mechanicals and their ideas of what a play should be.

certain for sure

This man … rough-cast (Snout is dressed to look like a wall, with a costume made of rough plaster and limestone)

sunder keep apart

lanthorn lantern

did … think no scorn were not ashamed

hight is called

affright frighten

mantle cloak

fall drop

Whereat at which, and then

broached stabbed

tarrying waiting

in mulberry shade in the shade of a mulberry bush

twain two

THESEUS His speech was like a tangled chain, nothing impaired, but all disordered. Who is next?

Enter with a Trumpeter before them [BOTTOM *as*] *Pyramus,* [FLUTE *as*] *Thisbe,* [SNOUT *as*] *Wall,* [STARVELING *as*] *Moonshine and* [SNUG *as*] *Lion.*

QUINCE (*as Prologue*)
Gentles, perchance you wonder at this show,
But wonder on, till truth make all things plain.
This man is Pyramus, if you would know;
This beauteous lady Thisbe is, certain.
This man with lime and rough-cast doth present
Wall, that vile wall which did these lovers sunder;
And through Wall's chink, poor souls, they are content
To whisper – at the which let no man wonder.
This man with lanthorn, dog, and bush of thorn,
Presenteth Moonshine; for, if you will know,
By moonshine did these lovers think no scorn
To meet at Ninus' tomb, there, there to woo.
This grisly beast, which Lion hight by name,
The trusty Thisbe, coming first by night,
Did scare away, or rather did affright;
And as she fled, her mantle she did fall,
Which Lion vile with bloody mouth did stain.
Anon comes Pyramus, sweet youth and tall,
And finds his trusty Thisbe's mantle slain;
Whereat with blade, with bloody, blameful blade,
He bravely broached his boiling bloody breast;
And Thisbe, tarrying in mulberry shade,
His dagger drew, and died. For all the rest,
Let Lion, Moonshine, Wall, and lovers twain
At large discourse, while here they do remain.
Exeunt Quince, Bottom, Flute, Snug and Starveling

Snout, as the Wall, explains his role. Bottom, as Pyramus, enters and begins the play's action.

1 Snout's opportunity – Wall! (in pairs)

Snout gets his great opportunity to speak as Wall. After his speech in the script opposite, he has only two more lines in the play, so he will surely make the most of lines 153–62.

Take turns to step into role and deliver his speech. Make the most of the rhymes and the stage directions that are built in to the language.

Stagecraft

Character comments (in small groups)

Discuss, come to a consensus and write detailed answers to these two questions:

- How would you want the onstage audience to respond to Theseus's and Demetrius's sarcastic and patronising comments?
- How would you direct the onstage audience to create that response?

Language in the play

Bottom's up! (in pairs)

At last Bottom gets his chance to show what he can do. In every production of the play, he seizes it wholeheartedly and throws himself into the role of tragic hero.

Take turns to act out Bottom's first speech as Pyramus – the other person can be Wall. Bottom's speech is full of repetition of words, sounds and ideas, so use them to increase the comedy. Here are some hints:

- **'O'** Bottom's notion of a tragic hero is that he uses 'O' whenever he can – so make the most of those exclamations.
- **Rhymes** There are all kinds of rhymes in the speech, not simply at the ends of lines. Exploit them for comic effect.
- **Rhythms** The lines are very rhythmical: phrases or sentences echo each other. Bottom thinks he must do full justice to those rhythms, making sure his audience really hears them.
- **Words** Bottom wants to convince his audience that it is 'night', that he speaks to 'Wall' and that he's sad ('alack'). Emphasise!

interlude short play

sinister left

lime and hair used to plaster walls

partition wall (or section of a speech)

sensible capable of feeling

curse again curse back, since it is 'sensible' (alive)

fall pat turn out right

THESEUS I wonder if the lion be to speak?

DEMETRIUS No wonder, my lord; one lion may, when many asses do.

SNOUT (*as Wall*)

In this same interlude it doth befall
That I, one Snout by name, present a wall;
And such a wall as I would have you think
That had in it a crannied hole or chink,
Through which the lovers, Pyramus and Thisbe,
Did whisper often, very secretly.
This loam, this rough-cast, and this stone doth show
That I am that same wall; the truth is so.
And this the cranny is, right and sinister,
Through which the fearful lovers are to whisper.

THESEUS Would you desire lime and hair to speak better?

DEMETRIUS It is the wittiest partition that ever I heard discourse, my lord.

Enter [Bottom as] Pyramus.

THESEUS Pyramus draws near the wall; silence!

BOTTOM (*as Pyramus*)

O grim-looked night, O night with hue so black,
O night which ever art when day is not!
O night, O night, alack, alack, alack,
I fear my Thisbe's promise is forgot!
And thou, O wall, O sweet, O lovely wall,
That stand'st between her father's ground and mine,
Thou wall, O wall, O sweet and lovely wall,
Show me thy chink, to blink through with mine eyne.
[*Wall parts his fingers.*]
Thanks, courteous wall; Jove shield thee well for this!
But what see I? No Thisbe do I see.
O wicked wall, through whom I see no bliss,
Cursed be thy stones for thus deceiving me!

THESEUS The wall, methinks, being sensible, should curse again.

BOTTOM No, in truth sir, he should not. 'Deceiving me' is Thisbe's cue. She is to enter now, and I am to spy her through the wall. You shall see it will fall pat as I told you. Yonder she comes.

Thisbe and Pyramus declare their love for each other through the chink in the wall, and agree to meet at 'Ninny's tomb'.

1 Mistakes (in small groups)

Keep a running tally of everything the Mechanicals get wrong in the performance. The audience watching on stage is of a higher social status than the Mechanicals, and would be better and more classically educated. Discuss how they would react to each mistake.

2 Third wheel (in threes)

Snout, as Wall, is listening in to the love talk, so his reactions to what he hears and sees are important. Talk together about his possible responses. Then discuss Flute's adopted 'female' voice and actions, and Bottom's over-the-top acting and mispronunciations. Remember that the aim is to make the 'real' (not onstage) audience laugh. Get up and act the lines in different ways.

Compare how the two productions shown on this page have chosen to present this moment. Think about the decisions regarding costumes, set, hair and make-up, and the impact those decisions might have had on an audience.

and if

Think … wilt take it as you like

thy lover's grace indeed your lover

Limander … Helen (these should be Leander and Hero, two legendary lovers)

trusty faithful

Fates goddesses who control people's lives

Shafalus … Procrus (another mistake – Flute means the legendary lovers Cephalus and Procris)

Ninny's tomb (Bottom repeats the mistake that Flute made during their rehearsal in Act 3)

Tide come

Enter [Flute as] Thisbe.

FLUTE (*as Thisbe*)
O wall, full often hast thou heard my moans,
For parting my fair Pyramus and me.
My cherry lips have often kissed thy stones,
Thy stones with lime and hair knit up in thee.

BOTTOM (*as Pyramus*)
I see a voice; now will I to the chink,
To spy and I can hear my Thisbe's face.
Thisbe!

FLUTE (*as Thisbe*)
My love! Thou art my love, I think?

BOTTOM (*as Pyramus*)
Think what thou wilt, I am thy lover's grace,
And like Limander am I trusty still.

FLUTE (*as Thisbe*)
And I like Helen, till the Fates me kill.

BOTTOM (*as Pyramus*)
Not Shafalus to Procrus was so true.

FLUTE (*as Thisbe*)
As Shafalus to Procrus, I to you.

BOTTOM (*as Pyramus*)
O, kiss me through the hole of this vile wall!

FLUTE (*as Thisbe*)
I kiss the wall's hole, not your lips at all.

BOTTOM (*as Pyramus*)
Wilt thou at Ninny's tomb meet me straightway?

FLUTE (*as Thisbe*)
Tide life, tide death, I come without delay.
[*Exeunt Bottom and Flute in different directions*]

Write about it

A silly, ridiculous play? (in small groups)

Hippolyta says, 'This is the silliest stuff that ever I heard.' Her comment is echoed by Samuel Pepys, the famous diarist, who said when he saw the play in 1662: 'We saw *Midsummer Night's Dreame*, which I have never seen before, nor shall ever again, for it is the most insipid ridiculous play that I ever saw in my life.' Theseus replies to Hippolyta, 'The best in this kind are but shadows'.

a Talk together and note down your ideas in response to the following three questions:

- How do you feel about Hippolyta's and Pepys's views?
- What are some possible meanings of Theseus's remark?
- What might Shakespeare have replied to Pepys if he had had the chance?

b On your own, write a letter from Pepys to Shakespeare criticising the play. Swap your letter with the person sitting next to you. Write Shakespeare's response to that person's letter.

Stagecraft

Snug the lion

Design a costume for Snug. Remember that the Mechanicals are amateurs who have never put on a play before. How professional do you think the costume should be? Look at the costumes in the images on this and previous pages as a starting point.

dischargèd so completed, finished with

mural wall

wilful ready

shadows dreams, visions

fell fierce

dam mother (lioness)

fox … goose the lion was supposed to be brave, the fox cunning (with 'discretion') and the goose stupid

SNOUT (*as Wall*)
Thus have I, Wall, my part dischargèd so;
And being done, thus Wall away doth go. *Exit*

THESEUS Now is the mural down between the two neighbours.

DEMETRIUS No remedy, my lord, when walls are so wilful to hear without warning.

HIPPOLYTA This is the silliest stuff that ever I heard.

THESEUS The best in this kind are but shadows; and the worst are no worse, if imagination amend them.

HIPPOLYTA It must be your imagination then, and not theirs.

THESEUS If we imagine no worse of them than they of themselves, they may pass for excellent men. Here come two noble beasts in, a man and a lion.

Enter [*Snug as*] *Lion and* [*Starveling as*] *Moonshine.*

SNUG (*as Lion*)
You ladies, you whose gentle hearts do fear
The smallest monstrous mouse that creeps on floor,
May now, perchance, both quake and tremble here,
When Lion rough in wildest rage doth roar.
Then know that I as Snug the joiner am
A lion fell, nor else no lion's dam;
For if I should as lion come in strife
Into this place, 'twere pity on my life.

THESEUS A very gentle beast, and of a good conscience.

DEMETRIUS The very best at a beast, my lord, that e'er I saw.

LYSANDER This lion is a very fox for his valour.

THESEUS True; and a goose for his discretion.

DEMETRIUS Not so, my lord; for his valour cannot carry his discretion; and the fox carries the goose.

THESEUS His discretion, I am sure, cannot carry his valour; for the goose carries not the fox. It is well: leave it to his discretion, and let us listen to the moon.

Starveling, Moonshine, manages to explain his role, despite the comments of the onstage audience. Thisbe arrives, only to be frightened away by the lion.

1 An unruly – and snobbish – audience? (in sevens)

The onstage audience seems to be getting out of hand. Starveling finds his performance is not appreciated. Take parts and read through lines 228–55 several times. Consider how Starveling says his lines 242–4. Is he irritated by the audience, intimidated by them or bored with the whole thing?

Language in the play

Imagining the moon (in pairs)

The image of the moon is common throughout *A Midsummer Night's Dream.*

a With a partner, choose five references to the moon in the play and analyse them in detail. Start with the two quotations below, and find three more by revisiting Acts 1 to 4.

Another moon – but O, methinks, how slow
This old moon wanes! She lingers my desires' (Act 1 Scene 1, lines 3–4)

Ill met by moonlight, proud Titania!' (Act 2 Scene 1, line 60)

b Write a short paragraph on what you think the moon might represent in this play. Why is it such an important image?

2 From imagining to creating

Because of the recurrent use of moon imagery, and because much of the action takes place at night, the moon is frequently used as a key element of set design and lighting effects in Acts 2, 3 and 4. Using the photograph above as a starting point, develop an idea of your own for physically integrating the moon into the play. The use of the moon in set design could present an amusing contrast with Starveling's lantern in this scene.

horns on his head the sign of a cuckold (someone whose wife has been unfaithful)

crescent waxing moon (growing larger)

already in snuff already snuffed out

aweary tired of

wane decline

Well moused (the lion is like a cat with a mouse – the mantle)

worries harasses, bites

STARVELING (*as Moonshine*)
This lanthorn doth the hornèd moon present –

DEMETRIUS He should have worn the horns on his head.

THESEUS He is no crescent, and his horns are invisible within the circumference.

STARVELING (*as Moonshine*)
This lanthorn doth the hornèd moon present;
Myself the man i'th'moon do seem to be –

THESEUS This is the greatest error of all the rest; the man should be put into the lantern. How is it else the man i'th'moon?

DEMETRIUS He dares not come there, for the candle; for you see it is already in snuff.

HIPPOLYTA I am aweary of this moon. Would he would change!

THESEUS It appears by his small light of discretion that he is in the wane; but yet in courtesy, in all reason, we must stay the time.

LYSANDER Proceed, Moon.

STARVELING All that I have to say is to tell you that the lanthorn is the moon, I the man i'th'moon, this thorn bush my thorn bush, and this dog my dog.

DEMETRIUS Why, all these should be in the lantern, for all these are in the moon. But silence: here comes Thisbe.

Enter [*Flute as*] *Thisbe.*

FLUTE (*as Thisbe*)
This is old Ninny's tomb. Where is my love?

SNUG (*as Lion*) O!

Lion roars. Thisbe runs off [*dropping her mantle*]

DEMETRIUS Well roared, Lion!

THESEUS Well run, Thisbe!

HIPPOLYTA Well shone, Moon! Truly, the moon shines with a good grace.

THESEUS Well moused, Lion!

DEMETRIUS And then came Pyramus –

LYSANDER And so the lion vanished.

[*Lion worries Thisbe's mantle, and exit*]

Pyramus enters full of expectation. He then sees Thisbe's blood-stained mantle, and calls for his own death.

1 Bottom struts his stuff (in small groups)

Now Bottom really gets the chance to display his acting skills. His speech in the script opposite and his lines 275–90 later in the scene are all part of the same sequence. First, get some experience of his whole performance by taking turns to speak as Bottom from line 256 to 290. Use the suggestions in the 'Language' box on page 128 and below to help you make the episode as funny as possible.

- **Humour** Shakespeare makes Bottom's attempts at acting humorous partly through his overuse of alliteration: 'gracious, golden, glittering gleams'. Make sure he emphasises all those hard 'g's.
- **Iambic pentameter** (see p. 164) Bottom begins with four lines in the traditional style of tragic heroes: lines with five beats. He will make sure that his audience appreciates that he knows his classics. Ensure that five emphatic stresses come over in each line. You will find he does just the same in his next speech, in lines 275–90.
- **Doggerel** Bottom does not keep up the 'high style' of his beginning. He changes to the very simple rhythms of two or three beats to a line. Again, take every opportunity to bring out those rhythms.

2 Romeo and Juliet – a parody?

As you work on the Mechanicals' play, keep thinking about whether Shakespeare is mocking romantic narratives, such as his own *Romeo and Juliet* perhaps, which he wrote around the same time as *A Midsummer Night's Dream*. Watch for romantic clichés in the remainder of the Mechanicals' play.

▼ **The deaths of Romeo and Juliet.**

dole reason for sadness

Furies avenging goddesses (usually depicted as three sisters who would punish crimes; both the Furies and the Fates link to ideas of fate, destiny and divine or supernatural intervention in real life)

Fates … thread and thrum goddesses who spin out the threads of people's lives and end them by cutting the thread and thrum (tuft on a thread)

Quail destroy

quell kill

passion suffering, violent outburst

Beshrew my heart exclamation, like 'Bless my soul'

Enter [Bottom as] Pyramus.

BOTTOM (*as Pyramus*)
Sweet moon, I thank thee for thy sunny beams;
I thank thee, moon, for shining now so bright;
For by thy gracious, golden, glittering gleams
I trust to take of truest Thisbe sight.
But stay – O spite!
But mark, poor Knight,
What dreadful dole is here?
Eyes, do you see?
How can it be?
O dainty duck, O dear!
Thy mantle good –
What, stained with blood?
Approach, ye Furies fell!
O Fates, come, come,
Cut thread and thrum,
Quail, crush, conclude, and quell.

THESEUS This passion, and the death of a dear friend, would go near to make a man look sad.

HIPPOLYTA Beshrew my heart, but I pity the man.

Pyramus stabs himself, and has a prolonged death. As the audience comments on the acting, Thisbe enters.

1 Bottom's great moment (in pairs)

Look back at the suggestions on page 136 for performing Bottom's final speech. When you have read them, take turns with your partner to play Bottom in Pyramus's death scene (lines 275–90). Make the most of the opportunity for physical humour, throwing yourself into the role and going thoroughly over the top. On stage, Bottom often mistakes right for left as he searches for his heart. He takes a very long time to deliver his final line, milking every 'die' for laughs. Usually, actors show how much Bottom is enjoying his moment on stage and how he is loath to leave it and 'die'.

Characters

An ass by any other name?

Yet again, someone implies that Bottom is an 'ass' (line 294). With a name like Bottom, and having an ass's head at one point, this perception of his character is pretty clear. Think about what Bottom says and does throughout the play, and make a list of reasons why Bottom is – or isn't – an ass. Find quotations for and against.

frame create

deflowered destroyed the innocence of

pap breast

die (line 291) one of a pair of dice

ace (one) is the lowest throw (Demetrius puns on Bottom's use of 'die')

passion suffering, passionate outburst

mote tiny particle

balance scale

means, videlicet moans, makes a formal legal complaint

BOTTOM (*as Pyramus*)
O wherefore, Nature, didst thou lions frame,
Since lion vile hath here deflowered my dear?
Which is – no, no – which was the fairest dame
That lived, that loved, that liked, that looked with cheer.
Come tears, confound!
Out sword, and wound
The pap of Pyramus,
Ay, that left pap,
Where heart doth hop:
Thus die I, thus, thus, thus! [*Stabs himself.*]
Now am I dead,
Now am I fled;
My soul is in the sky.
Tongue, lose thy light;
Moon, take thy flight;
[*Exit Starveling*]
Now die, die, die, die, die. [*He dies.*]

DEMETRIUS No die, but an ace for him; for he is but one.

LYSANDER Less than an ace, man; for he is dead, he is nothing.

THESEUS With the help of a surgeon he might yet recover, and yet prove an ass.

HIPPOLYTA How chance Moonshine is gone before Thisbe comes back and finds her lover?

THESEUS She will find him by starlight.

Enter [*Flute as*] *Thisbe.*

Here she comes and her passion ends the play.

HIPPOLYTA Methinks she should not use a long one for such a Pyramus; I hope she will be brief.

DEMETRIUS A mote will turn the balance, which Pyramus, which Thisbe is the better: he for a man, God warrant us; she for a woman, God bless us.

LYSANDER She hath spied him already, with those sweet eyes.

DEMETRIUS And thus she means, videlicet –

Thisbe realises Pyramus is dead and kills herself. Bottom asks if the duke wants an epilogue or a dance. Theseus settles on the country dance.

▲ **Look at the man playing Flute (Thisbe) in the photograph above. Think about whether this image works well, and what Flute might be like if played by very different-looking actors. The actors in the pictures on page 130, for example, look much more feminine.**

1 'Adieu, adieu, adieu!' (in pairs)

a Compare and contrast the death scene of Pyramus with that of Thisbe. Consider how costume, props and facial expressions can be used to heighten humour.

b How much sadness or pathos would you like to convey? Discuss how the characters of Bottom and Flute can be developed through their performances as the doomed lovers. In some productions, members of the onstage audience feel more involved at this point and enter into the play more sympathetically than they did earlier.

2 Hot-seat questions (in pairs, then whole class)

The Mechanicals complete their play. What questions would you like to ask Bottom and Quince at this point about the details of the play, their performances and the audience?

- In pairs, agree on your most important two questions, one for each of these two characters.
- One member of the class plays Bottom, and one Quince. In character, they each have to answer one question from each pair.

lily lips (surely lips should be red, not lily white?)

cherry cherry-red

eyes were green as leeks (green is a colour associated with jealousy, not love, so this is another inappropriate and comic image from Thisbe; all the misapplication of colour is part of the comedy of this scene)

sisters three the Fates (see glossary on p. 136)

hands as pale as milk (a common image for a lady's skin)

gore blood

shore shorn, cut

thread of silk lifeline

imbrue stab, make bloody

left left alive

Bergomask country dance

notably discharged admirably performed

FLUTE (*as Thisbe*)
Asleep, my love?
What, dead, my dove?
O Pyramus, arise.
Speak, speak! Quite dumb?
Dead, dead? A tomb
Must cover thy sweet eyes.
These lily lips,
This cherry nose,
These yellow cowslip cheeks
Are gone, are gone.
Lovers, make moan;
His eyes were green as leeks.
O sisters three,
Come, come to me
With hands as pale as milk;
Lay them in gore,
Since you have shore
With shears his thread of silk.
Tongue, not a word!
Come, trusty sword,
Come blade, my breast imbrue! [*Stabs herself.*]
And farewell, friends.
Thus Thisbe ends –
Adieu, adieu, adieu! [*Dies.*]

THESEUS Moonshine and Lion are left to bury the dead.

DEMETRIUS Ay, and Wall, too.

BOTTOM [*Starting up, as Flute does also.*] No, I assure you, the wall is down that parted their fathers. Will it please you to see the epilogue, or to hear a Bergomask dance between two of our company?

THESEUS No epilogue, I pray you; for your play needs no excuse. Never excuse; for when the players are all dead, there need none to be blamed. Marry, if he that write it had played Pyramus and hanged himself in Thisbe's garter, it would have been a fine tragedy: and so it is, truly, and very notably discharged. But come, your Bergomask; let your epilogue alone.

The Mechanicals dance, the duke instructs everyone to go to bed, and Puck enters. He speaks of the night, the time when the fairies play.

1 Puck's night-time world (in pairs)

Listen as your teacher reads Puck's speech (lines 349–68) aloud twice through. Individually, draw what you consider to be the major night-time images. Share your final design with a partner. Have you picked up the same images or focused on different ones? Describe the mood presented by your images. The results could be used to make a classroom display.

Language in the play

'Enter PUCK [carrying a broom]' (in pairs)

I am sent with broom before
To sweep the dust behind the door.

Robin Goodfellow was thought to sweep the house at midnight as a good turn, and often maids would put out a bowl of milk as thanks. It is not clear here whether Puck is clearing away the dust or just sweeping it behind the door and then leaving it there. With your partner, discuss the significance and purpose of this metaphor at this point in the play.

Write about it

Three worlds – three accounts (in threes)

The mortals have left, and the fairy world begins its entrance. One member of the group chooses to be one of the lovers, another is one of the Mechanicals and the third is a member of the court. Each writes a diary account of the evening. Concentrate on perceptions, thoughts and feelings rather than simply describing events. Take turns to read out your accounts.

iron tongue … told the bell was struck

overwatched watched over

palpable-gross obviously uncouth

beguiled charmed or enchanted

heavy gait laboured passage, slow pace

A fortnight … solemnity we have two weeks of ceremonies and festivities

heavy tired

foredone worn out

wasted brands burnt logs

triple Hecate's team the moon's chariot

frolic merry

hallowed saintly

[*The company return; two of them dance, then exeunt Bottom, Flute and their fellows.*]

The iron tongue of midnight hath told twelve.
Lovers, to bed; 'tis almost fairy time.
I fear we shall outsleep the coming morn
As much as we this night have overwatched.
This palpable-gross play hath well beguiled
The heavy gait of night. Sweet friends, to bed.
A fortnight hold we this solemnity
In nightly revels and new jollity.

Exeunt

Enter PUCK [*carrying a broom*].

PUCK Now the hungry lion roars,
And the wolf behowls the moon,
Whilst the heavy ploughman snores,
All with weary task foredone.
Now the wasted brands do glow,
Whilst the screech-owl, screeching loud,
Puts the wretch that lies in woe
In remembrance of a shroud.
Now it is the time of night
That the graves, all gaping wide,
Every one lets forth his sprite
In the church-way paths to glide.
And we fairies, that do run
By the triple Hecate's team
From the presence of the sun,
Following darkness like a dream,
Now are frolic; not a mouse
Shall disturb this hallowed house.
I am sent with broom before
To sweep the dust behind the door.

Oberon and Titania enter with their fairies. Oberon instructs them to go through the house, blessing the three couples with loving marriages and 'perfect' children.

1 Blessing mortal marriages (in pairs)

Oberon delivers the blessing of the fairy world on the three marriages. He speaks in four-beat rhythm, quite different from the verse of the court and the prose of the Mechanicals. His blessing draws on country myths and folk tales. Every culture has its own blessings, and you may wish to research these. The following is a blessing on marriage and children from *The Book of Common Prayer* (1662):

> *We beseech thee, assist with thy blessing these two persons, that they may both be fruitful in procreation of children, and also live together so long in godly love and honesty, that they may see their children christianly and virtuously brought up, to thy praise and honour; through Jesus Christ our Lord.*

With a partner, decide how Oberon should speak his lines in the script. The mythical and religious connections suggest a serious and reverential approach, but the song and dance imply a lighter tone. Decide as directors how you would advise your actor on his line delivery and actions.

Themes

From conflict to 'sweet peace' (in small groups)

Compare the speeches in the script opposite with the conflicts of the opening scene and the conflicts in the wood. The play has dramatised problems in the relationships between women and men. What has brought them to 'sweet peace' now?

a For each couple, describe their conflicts and explain how they have been resolved.

b Write a short dialogue between one of the couples, in which they look back at what has happened to them over the last two days. End their conversation with their thoughts about what the future holds. (You may also want to look at 'Conflict', p. 151.)

ditty song

trippingly gracefully

by rote by heart, memorised

stray wander away

best bride-bed the wedding bed of Theseus and Hippolyta

issue children

true faithful

blots of nature's hand bodily features that were considered unnatural birth defects, such as birthmarks, moles and hare lips

mark prodigious birthmark with an evil omen

Despisèd in nativity loathed at birth

consecrate bless

take his gait go his way

several separate

Enter [OBERON *and* TITANIA,] *the King and Queen of Fairies, with all their train.*

OBERON
Through the house give glimmering light
By the dead and drowsy fire;
Every elf and fairy sprite
Hop as light as bird from briar,
And this ditty after me
Sing, and dance it trippingly.

TITANIA
First rehearse your song by rote,
To each word a warbling note;
Hand in hand with fairy grace
Will we sing and bless this place.

Song [*and dance*].

OBERON
Now until the break of day
Through this house each fairy stray.
To the best bride-bed will we,
Which by us shall blessèd be;
And the issue there create
Ever shall be fortunate.
So shall all the couples three
Ever true in loving be,
And the blots of nature's hand
Shall not in their issue stand.
Never mole, harelip, nor scar,
Nor mark prodigious, such as are
Despisèd in nativity,
Shall upon their children be.
With this field-dew consecrate,
Every fairy take his gait,
And each several chamber bless
Through this palace with sweet peace;
And the owner of it blessed
Ever shall in safety rest.
Trip away, make no stay;
Meet me all by break of day.

Exeunt [*all but Puck*]

Puck, on his own now, asks for the audience to think of the play as their dream. He promises improved performances and asks for the audience's approval.

Stagecraft

Puck's farewell (in pairs)

a The best thing to do with Puck's farewell is to speak it. Take turns with your partner to deliver the lines. Help each other by suggesting different ways of increasing dramatic effect.

b Think carefully about positioning this soliloquy in relation to the audience. Try a close and intimate approach and then a more distant, formal one. Present your preferred version to the class.

c As Puck's speech closes the play, try to describe the final mood on stage in three words.

shadows fairies

No more yielding producing no more profit

Gentles (Puck politely addresses the audience as gentlefolk)

reprehend reprimand

mend improve

'scape the serpent's tongue escape the audience hissing (because of a poor performance)

Give me your hands applaud

Robin shall restore amends Puck will, in return, make amends for a poor performance

Characters

Who else might speak to the audience?

Puck speaks directly to the audience, which in Shakespeare's time would either hiss ('the serpent's tongue') or clap ('Give me your hands') at the end of plays. Plays often ended with a request to the audience to clap (and not hiss). Is Puck the right character to end the play and ask the audience for their applause?

a Suggest why Shakespeare gives him the final word, even though he has been so mischievous and negative about humans in the play: 'Lord, what fools these mortals be', 'The shallowest thick-skin of that barren sort'.

b If you had to choose a different character to speak the final words, who would it be and why? Write a paragraph on your suggestions and reasoning. What might your alternative character say to the audience at the end of the play?

PUCK [*To the audience*]

If we shadows have offended,
Think but this, and all is mended:
That you have but slumbered here
While these visions did appear;
And this weak and idle theme,
No more yielding but a dream,
Gentles, do not reprehend;
If you pardon, we will mend.
And, as I am an honest Puck,
If we have unearnèd luck
Now to 'scape the serpent's tongue
We will make amends ere long,
Else the Puck a liar call.
So, good night unto you all.
Give me your hands, if we be friends,
And Robin shall restore amends. [*Exit*]

Looking back at the play

Activities for groups or individuals

1 Presenting Puck

Compare the photographs on this page with other images of Puck in the book. Talk with the person next to you about what you think works well in each image and what you would change. How would you present Puck in your own production of *A Midsummer Night's Dream*?

2 Puck as symbol

'We cannot possibly deal with Puck as a realistic character.' Say whether or not you agree with this statement, then suggest what issues and themes Shakespeare is exploring through this character. Pool your ideas in a small group in the form of a spider diagram.

3 Important to you – why?

Write down what you consider to be the ten most important quotations in the play. Compare your list with a partner's, giving reasons for your choices.

4 Sixty-second challenge

In pairs, write a quick version of the play, with all the main characters (you may want to cut some of the minor ones), that lasts one minute. You will have to prioritise the key moments and reduce each of them to its fundamental words or message. The class could perform the most successful attempt.

5 What were Shakespeare's views?

What do you think were Shakespeare's own views on his groups of characters? Where do you think his sympathies lie? Does he present one group more positively than another? What attitudes, values and ideas does he appear to be addressing through the construction of his characters? Talk about their behaviour, language, interactions, values and development during the play. Rank the groups of characters in order, from the one Shakespeare presents most positively, to the least, with your rationale.

6 Unpleasant moments?

Although this play falls firmly into the comedy category of Shakespearean plays, it has its bleak and unpleasant scenes and images. Identify particular moments in the play that you think could be seen as disturbing. Present your findings in pictorial or diagrammatic format. Add comments explaining how the examples you have chosen could be played as both nightmarish and comic, and how important messages are being conveyed through these serious and perhaps disturbing scenes.

7 A futuristic all-action movie

You are a screenwriter who has been commissioned by a Hollywood director to write a film version of *A Midsummer Night's Dream*. The director is intrigued by the surreal and mystical nature of the play. He wants it to be set in the future and modelled on such blockbuster movies as *Avatar*, *Prometheus* and *Cloud Atlas*. In pairs, work on one short scene and invent some suggestions to present at a script conference.

8 And finally …

You have the opportunity to meet William Shakespeare and can ask only one question about this play. What would be your question? Write it down, taking care that it is thoughtful, intelligent and well expressed. Remember that Shakespeare is the most influential and famous playwright of all time.

Perspectives and themes

What is the play about?

A Midsummer Night's Dream is a play about love, and it shows clearly that 'the course of true love never did run smooth'. When used as a technical term in drama, the word **comedy** doesn't just mean that something is funny. A Shakespearean comedy is a play where everything starts in chaos but ends in harmony, as opposed to its opposite, the **tragedy**, where a situation that seems harmonious to start with ends in chaos. *A Midsummer Night's Dream* is a comedy, so traditionally should end happily, with problems solved along the way. At times the play presents threatening moments for its central characters, with scenes of dramatic tension, hurt and humiliation interspersed with farce and comedy.

The play begins with plans to celebrate a wedding. Theseus, Duke of Athens, and Hippolyta, Queen of the Amazons, have been at war but now are to marry to ensure future peace. This scene is interrupted by Egeus, a court official with a problem that he demands Theseus should solve. His daughter is refusing to marry the man he has chosen for her. Much of the rest of the play focuses on the attempts of the various lovers to sort out their complex relationship problems.

The play has three main groups of characters:

- Four **lovers** (and Hippolyta and Theseus) live in and around the court of Athens. They are primarily concerned with their love lives and how to achieve happiness. The lovers are very young, and the action of the play will, to some extent, see them grow up and become more perceptive.
- **The Mechanicals** are ordinary working men; friends interested in amateur dramatics who are keen to perform a play before the duke at his wedding. If their play is chosen they will earn respect and 'sixpence a day' for life, ensuring financial security.
- **The fairies** have their foundations in myth, legend and superstition and can be interpreted in a wide variety of ways. They are often the most memorable characters because of the imaginative nature of the characterisation and the richness of their language.

Three storylines run through the play:

- The problematic story of the lovers – Hermia and Lysander, and Helena and Demetrius – that revolves around their dramatic attempts to avoid parental interference and marry happily.
- The Mechanicals' endeavour to rehearse their play: Bottom, their lead actor, becomes involved in the third plot in a relationship with the fairy queen.
- The conflict between Oberon and Titania, the king and queen of the fairies, is presented as a fight for power and control. Oberon and his attendant, Puck, become involved in the lovers' complex interactions.

These storylines all unite in Act 2, as Shakespeare cleverly contrives to have the characters in the same wood on the same night. The lovers are never aware of the fairies, who cause greater turmoil in their relationships before order is restored. The Mechanicals have contact with the fairy world, with Bottom used in Oberon's humiliation of Titania. The lovers do not see the Mechanicals until the final act, when they watch them perform their version of *Pyramus and Thisbe*, which partly parodies the lovers' own situation.

Themes

Another way of answering the question 'What is *A Midsummer Night's Dream* about?' is to identify the themes of the play. Themes are ideas or concepts of fundamental importance that recur throughout the play, linking together plot, characters and language. Themes echo, reinforce and comment upon each other and the whole play in interesting ways. Complex themes are woven through the play and often interconnect with each other – for example, the theme of love is explored alongside that of patriarchy. Hermia loves Lysander but is being prevented from marrying him by the controlling influence and dominant voice of her father, Egeus.

As you can see, themes are not individual categories but a mix of ideas and concerns that are interrelated in complex ways. When discussing, analysing and writing about the play you should aim to explore the way these themes cross over and illuminate each other, rather than simply listing each of the themes.

You might also like to think about the way the themes work at three different levels: the individual level (psychological or personal); the social level (linked to society and nation); and the natural level (the natural or supernatural world). *A Midsummer Night's Dream* is a play about love and relationships, and this theme weaves together all three levels.

Conflict

Shakespeare dramatises the conflict in each relationship. Egeus attempts to force his will on his daughter, but she defies him. Helena's love for Demetrius is unrequited, and in her hurt and bitterness she betrays her best friend. Driven by frustration, Demetrius behaves aggressively towards Helena. Hippolyta and Theseus's relationship begins with the conflict of war, and Oberon and Titania are at odds, causing disruption to the natural world. The mythical figures Pyramus and Thisbe die for love of each other.

By the end of Act 3, the four young lovers are at each other's throats. Helena and Hermia quarrel in a spiteful, abusive way and Lysander and Demetrius try to kill each other. Their interaction is punctuated by moments of confusion ('I am amazed, and know not what to say'), mockery ('they have conjoined all three / To fashion this false sport in spite of me') and pain ('Can you do me greater harm than hate?').

However, the lovers are all happily united in the end, and the fairies ensure future harmony:

So shall all the couples three
Ever true in loving be

- **Discuss and make notes on how each pair of lovers in the play provides similarities and contrasts, and highlights certain themes (don't forget Titania and Bottom, and Pyramus and Thisbe). You may want to organise your responses in a table so that comparisons and patterns are clearer.**

Love and marriage

The play looks at the problems facing lovers and the obstacles placed in the way of true happiness. Shakespeare begins with Theseus's 'nuptial hour' that 'draws on apace', but Theseus's tender comments on his 'desires' and happiness are soon tempered when the audience realises that he has won Hippolyta 'with his sword'. However, although there are lovers' quarrels, misunderstandings and scenes of cruelty and bitterness, the audience is encouraged to laugh at the plight of lovers and feels secure in the knowledge that it will all end happily. We see how love makes people look foolish, blind, fickle and desperate. At the end we see that 'Jack shall have Jill' and 'naught shall go ill'. Ironically, this is achieved through the intervention of the fairy king rather than the lovers' own good sense.

A closely related theme is the difference between 'doting' and 'love', something like the distinction between fancying someone and loving them. The play also presents love as a kind of madness, showing that 'reason and love keep little company together'. The variety of relationships provides parallels and contrasts. Shakespeare presents the audience with four couples whose relationships need resolving, allowing a range of other themes to be explored – particularly conflict and change.

Order and disorder

The play explores the need for a balance between the rational and irrational, between rules and magic, in the interests of love, harmony and creativity. The order of the Athenian Court, with its cultural restrictions, strict hierarchies and strict legal systems is rejected by the lovers as they escape its limitations to seek freedom and a more accepting world. The Mechanicals also attempt to escape from their secure and ordered lives into the make-believe world of amateur dramatics. When the fairy world meets the mortal world, it creates a fever of disorder and confusion.

Appearance and reality

Many of Shakespeare's plays show how people and events are often not as they seem. Puck transforms Bottom into an ass (although Puck's choice does to some extent reflect an aspect of Bottom's nature). Later, Puck meddles with the lover's feelings, causing confusion: 'I am amazed and know not what to say.' Even at the end, when their lives have been restored to a semblance of normality, neither the lovers nor Bottom understands what has happened and cannot distinguish between their waking lives and dreams. This theme is explored comically in the Mechanicals' flight of fancy in their production of *Pyramus and Thisbe*.

Gender tensions

It is possible to interpret *A Midsummer Night's Dream* as a play about women defying men. The female characters do not conform to the accepted norm of subservience. The action begins with an Amazonian queen who has battled with Theseus and lost. Even though they are betrothed, their relationship continues to show signs of conflict. Hermia stands up to her father and insists on her right to marry the man she loves. Helena proclaims her unrequited love to the world in a way that does not follow expected behaviour, and she spends much of the play chasing Demetrius through the woods at night. The tensions have echoes in the fairy world, where Titania is totally unwilling to submit to Oberon's demands and defies him as long as she is able.

The conventional ending with the women accepting their place as compliant to the will of the men may jar with modern sensibilities, but would have been familiar to Shakespeare's contemporaries in a world where men had more power than women. Elizabeth I was a real exception, introducing a new concept of monarchy where a woman could be a successful ruler.

Motifs

Motifs are recurring elements and patterns of imagery that support the play's themes.

Nature, represented through the magical world of the forest, is placed in contrast with the civilised court of Theseus. The natural world is disrupted by the disharmony between the fairy king and queen: 'And through this distemperature we see / The seasons alter'.

The moon is used to reflect change, disruption and unpredictability: 'Therefore the moon, the governess of floods, / Pale in her anger, washes all the air'.

Sleep and dreams in the play take us to mysterious places. They are states of innocence and vulnerability, and cause confusion and the blurring of boundaries between fantasy and reality: 'God's my life, stolen hence, and left me asleep! I have had a most rare vision. I have had a dream.'

The **eyes** are signs of perception and perspective: 'Reason becomes the marshal to my will / And leads me to your eyes, where I o'erlook / Love's stories written in love's richest book'. They symbolically provide access to the heart, and are 'windows on the soul'.

Shakespeare uses the idea of putting on a play and **playing roles** to represent magical transformation and the importance of the imagination. It is also an ironic comment that plays are not real: 'you have but slumbered here / While these visions did appear.'

Magic appears in the play as the unseen, the unpredictable, the irrational and inexplicable.

- **Choose five quotations where magic is being performed and explain how the magic develops and shapes some of the themes in the play in each example.**
- **Write a paragraph exploring Shakespeare's use of the motif of magic and its impact on the characters and an audience.**

The contexts of *A Midsummer Night's Dream*

Elizabeth I and her court

A Midsummer Night's Dream was written towards the end of the reign of Queen Elizabeth I. Elizabeth was Gloriana, the Virgin Queen who had taken on an almost mythical significance in the imagination of her subjects. Both Hippolyta and Titania embody certain aspects of Elizabeth's royal mystique. Hippolyta, as the beautiful 'Amazon queen', evokes Elizabeth's reputation for military prowess, as well as her political refusal to marry. Her navy had conquered the Spanish Armada and she had ruled for longer than any other monarch.

Elizabeth also has much in common with Titania. Shakespeare represents Titania as a great patroness of music, dancing and the arts, as was Elizabeth. Titania, the fairy queen of the play, clearly references the famous epic poem by Edmund Spenser, *The Faerie Queene*, written in 1590, which was an elaborate celebration of Elizabeth and her court.

The fairy 'court' and its rituals and relationships appear in many ways to mimic and perhaps parody those of the human duke, Theseus. Oberon's and Titania's roles as rulers with power, surrounded by their attendants, are strongly reminiscent of the world of mortal monarchs. Whether their conflicts, bitter words, licentiousness and jealousy present a commentary on the Elizabethan court is arguable, but this aspect of the play may serve as a cautionary tale on the consequences of immorality and corruption. Their behaviour certainly seems to mimic the worst excesses and spoilt manners of the aristocracy.

Although the play is full of possible references to her, there is no evidence that Queen Elizabeth ever saw *A Midsummer Night's Dream*. Some critics have suggested that the play contains a message to Elizabeth about how responsibility and power must be tempered by the natural laws of feeling and sensitivity.

Greek setting

The play is set in Athens, yet its characterisation and thematic development seems very English – particularly the presentation of the Mechanicals, their working background and their language. The Greek setting is used because the more cultured and educated of Shakespeare's audience would have recognised the allusions to mythological figures and made connections with the legends, which would have given the play serious literary and historical reference points. The historical setting also serves to 'disguise' possible connections with contemporary figures. This was important for Shakespeare who, along with all other playwrights, was dependent on sponsorships (individuals and businesses who contributed financially to the running and upkeep of theatres and theatre companies) and needed to protect himself from political interference and censorship.

Often in Shakespeare's plays, an ancient and cosmopolitan setting suggests order and reason. Certainly, Theseus's court runs on strict rules and social expectations. The forest, which Lysander and Hermia use to escape 'the sharp Athenian law', presents a stark contrast: reason and order have little place there.

Fairies and magic

The characters of Oberon and Puck have their foundations in mythology. The placing of the action on Midsummer's Eve connects them with pagan celebrations. Much of the play takes place at dusk and at night, when tradition held that fairies were at their most active. It is also the time when witches were said to harvest magical plants: it is during the night of Midsummer's Eve that Oberon instructs Puck to go in search for 'love-in-idleness', with its transformational emotional powers.

Puck is the fairy with the most traditional associations with myth and legend. Under Oberon's command, he plays the role of Cupid and attempts to put right the mortals' love dilemmas. Puck is introduced to the audience as 'Robin' at the start of Act 2. Robin Goodfellow was a mythological character who would have been familiar to an Elizabethan audience. However, the name Puck finds its origins in 'Puca', an old English term for a woodland spirit who was much feared by ordinary folk. 'Pouk' was a medieval name for the devil, so for Shakespeare's contemporaries Puck would have profound resonances – most of them ominous. In traditional stories, Robin Goodfellow was known as a 'hairy goat-man, horned and hoofed'. His connection with evil and mischief is clear. (Remind yourself of the image and notes on p. 55, and see also p. 158.)

May Day celebrations and English traditions

A Midsummer Night's Dream is one of Shakespeare's early 'festive comedies'. The play contains a fair amount of commentary on Shakespeare's contemporary English world. The title refers to an English holiday custom, Midsummer Eve – the night of the summer solstice at the end of June. On this evening, bonfires were lit and people would sit outdoors. The custom was to tell stories of fairies and witchcraft. The play also refers to 'the rite of May' – a similar English tradition that took place on the first night of May, when young people would sing and dance in the woods outside their towns. This was an occasion for flirtation and romantic dalliances. The play's title and setting recall English social and cultural traditions as well as suggesting superstitions, wild parties and making offerings to the gods.

At the time the play was written, these traditions had come under attack by the English Puritans, who thought that they were inappropriate and ungodly 'pagan' practices that encouraged lawlessness and immorality. The play's happy ending, after all its midsummer madness, implies Shakespeare's defence of rural folklore and customs. They are certainly presented as amusing and harmless. Egeus, the character closest to a killjoy, is silenced by Theseus at the end: 'I will overbear your will.' Philostrate, who disapproves of ordinary men's involvement in celebratory festivities, is shown to be similarly joyless.

The working man

In English towns, the economy did not concentrate on agriculture. Here, the people were either craftsmen or labourers, like the Mechanicals. Men earned their living as butchers, bakers, tailors, weavers, blacksmiths and carpenters. At this stage in the economic development of England, people did everything by hand. Those who did not produce their own goods focused on selling others' goods to earn a living.

Women in Elizabethan England

Although England had a female ruler, women were considered significantly inferior to men. Men held most power in the workplace and within the family. Women had little say about whom they married; a male relative (usually the father) chose a young women's future husband on the basis of status. A man who would bring increased prestige, money or social respectability to a family was considered to be a catch. This was an important fact of life for upper- or middle-class women, and Shakespeare gives this issue prominence by showing Egeus's determination that his daughter will marry the man of his choice. As with men, a girl's fate was bound up in her class and financial situation. A poor rural woman would toil hard on the land as well as bringing up the children and running the home.

A middle-class woman's life may have been more economically secure, but she had no independence and little personal power or control over the family's finances. Like women of other classes, she usually had to endure numerous pregnancies. Infant mortality was high, as was death in childbirth. A woman had no access to divorce and no rights to her own children. A woman was entirely at the mercy of her husband's nature.

Even upper-class women were totally dependent on men, and were used to forge alliances with other powerful or rich families through arranged marriages. If they did not marry, they depended on male relatives to support them. Their main roles in life were to marry well and to bear male heirs. This presented a dilemma for Elizabeth I: convention dictated that if she married, she would have to obey her husband. This may explain why she chose to remain unmarried.

It was, however, customary for upper-class girls to receive a good education. They were tutored at home and were expected to be proficient in languages, the classics, history and music, as well as the more domestic skills of needlework and household management. Elizabeth herself was an accomplished scholar. She shared her brother's tutors as a child and was better educated than most of the men at her court. By the age of eleven, Elizabeth was able to speak fluently in six languages – French, Greek, Latin, Spanish, Welsh and, of course, English.

Shakespeare's depiction of women in the play is interesting in light of this. Hermia is an upper-class girl, clearly intelligent and articulate, who decides to defy her father. Although she has moments of hardship and suffering, she ends up happily married to the man she has chosen.

- **Work in pairs, with one of you taking the part of Helena and the other Hippolyta. Re-read the scenes where these characters appear, and make notes on how Shakespeare presents them. Think about their language and ideas, the choices they make and the consequences of these choices on their lives. Together, consider whether this research gives you an insight into the lives of Elizabethan women.**
- **As a whole class, hold a discussion on the similarities and differences of life for women in the 1590s and in the early twenty-first century.**

Art and theatre

One of the most interesting aspects of *A Midsummer Night's Dream* is that the audience is unsure whether what they have seen is real, or whether they have just watched some kind of dream sequence. They feel the same sense of disorientation as Bottom and the lovers. This is, of course, precisely what Shakespeare wants to make clear – that the theatre is about the power of the imagination, a shared dream.

In the play within the play, the Mechanicals present their interpretation of *Pyramus and Thisbe*, a play they have made up themselves, which makes demands on the offstage audience's suspension of reality. The onstage audience's constant interruptions serve to highlight all that is unreal in a drama. Ironically, the Mechanicals are able to show total belief in their play. Much of the humour in their rehearsals and performance comes from their fumbled attempts to stage a classical, tragic story. Shakespeare focuses much of his plot on this 'theatre within a theatre'. This is partly a structural device to include scenes of pure physical and linguistic comedy, driven by well-meaning and serious but totally inept characters. It also causes the offstage audience to reflect on what makes great theatre and the roles of the actors and the audience in accomplishing this.

The performance of *Pyramus and Thisbe* – however delightful for the real audience at the theatre – clearly does not work for the onstage audience. Watching their reactions to the performance helps us to draw our own conclusions about why this is, and adds to our enjoyment.

Characters

Oberon

Oberon has his roots in a wide variety of European myths and legends, and it is unclear which of these influenced Shakespeare when drawing up this complex character. There is a fairy elf ruler called Alberich in ancient German mythology; his story, written in the thirteenth century, also revolves around war, love and marriage. The name Oberon was first seen in a thirteenth-century French tale of a fairy dwarf: the story tells of how this handsome dwarf helps the hero to succeed in winning a king's pardon.

In *A Midsummer Night's Dream*, the audience first learns from Puck of Oberon's anger towards Titania, and so is prepared for his dominant and adversarial presence on stage. Thematically, there are links between Oberon and Theseus. Both are powerful men who subdue the women they love. The mortal and the fairy worlds are presented as male-dominated societies. Titania accuses Oberon of amorous interest in a number of mythical women, including Hippolyta, who is described as being his former 'warrior love'. Quite often, Theseus and Oberon are played by the same actor, as are Hippolyta and Titania, which creates a connection in the mind of the audience. Oberon's interest in sexual relationships is a key part of his character. We also learn that he was involved with a country girl named Phillida (a mythical shepherdess known to be in a passionate but unrequited relationship) and disguised himself as a shepherd so that he could pursue her. He involves himself in the lovers' complex relationships and attends the blessing of their wedding beds at the end.

Oberon has impressive magical powers that make him – and Puck – fascinating to watch. The invisibility that enables them to overhear mortal talk can be presented as either amusing or sinister. Oberon's magic and Puck's ability to 'Put a girdle round about the earth' allows for the use of interesting visuals and special effects such as trapdoors, lighting effects, mirrors and hidden wires. The 'love-in-idleness' flower can be perceived as the absolute abuse of power, as it interferes with emotions, or as the ultimate righter of wrongs. The power the fairies have to create storms and ruin crops parallels a monarch's power to affect the lives of others, which emphasises the fact that influence must be accompanied by a sense of responsibility. It could also allude to the Elizabethan view that the supernatural world was able to interfere in the mortal world (good versus evil forces, reflected in chaos and harmony in nature).

Titania

Titania is presented as a regal figure, sure of her power and importance. She keeps a rival court to Oberon's, and has her own attendants. During her struggle with Oberon, she defies him and refuses to submit to his bullying. She certainly dominates their first encounter, leaving him spluttering threats after her: 'Thou shalt not from this grove / Till I torment thee for this injury.' She holds the stage dramatically for some time during her famous 'forgeries of jealousy' speech (Act 2 Scene 1, lines 81–117). This is the longest speech in the play, and through its powerful imagery the dominance and force of the fairy world, as well as the violence of their emotions, is made clear to the audience.

After Titania's initial assertive behaviour, Oberon succeeds in tormenting her. Her relationship with Oberon is obviously sexual, with constant accusations of jealousy and betrayal. Her punishment for not complying with her husband's wishes is to be made to fall in love with the transformed Bottom: 'What angel wakes me from my flowery bed?' This relationship is amusing because of the irony of a beautiful fairy queen believing herself in love with an arrogant, ugly labouring man who looks like an ass.

While retaining her authoritative nature – 'Out of this wood do not desire to go: / Thou shalt remain here, whether thou wilt or no.' – she is truly enraptured with her hairy-faced love. Her enslavement to her emotions is so absolute that even Oberon begins to pity her.

Titania has strong links with the natural world (see again her 'forgeries of jealousy' speech), and her language is full of natural and cosmic imagery.

By the end of the play she is reunited with Oberon and her role, with him, appears to be to bless the marriages of the newlywed mortals. However, in order to regain her own marital harmony she has had to suffer a cruel indignity and give in to Oberon's wishes. For a modern audience, Titania's capitulation to Oberon is surprising. (See 'Women in Elizabethan England', p. 154.)

Puck

Puck keeps Oberon amused with his antics: 'I jest to Oberon, and make him smile.' He is an enigmatic character, difficult to read and capable of being presented on the stage in a variety of ways. He is the first fairy introduced to the audience, and is variously described as a 'shrewd and knavish sprite' and 'that merry wanderer of the night.' He has been played by adult actors (male and female) as well as by children. As a character he is certainly a lot of fun; he indulges in great merriment at the expense of the humans with whom he comes into contact. He takes pleasure in people's indignities and misfortunes:

And those things do best please me
That befall prepost'rously.

Puck is Oberon's servant and their relationship appears affectionate: 'My gentle Puck', 'Welcome, wanderer.' However, Oberon is well aware of the true nature of his messenger's 'mad spirit' and will happily blame him when things go wrong:

This is thy negligence. Still thou mistak'st,
Or else committ'st thy knaveries wilfully.

Shakespeare appears to enjoy Puck, and uses him as a running commentary on the absurdities of the mortals. An audience can feel that Puck is right when he exclaims 'Lord, what fools these mortals be!' He has his parallel in the jesters in a real court, whose job was to entertain the monarch and courtiers with jokes, physical humour and observations on the stupidity of their behaviour. A court jester was often allowed to get away with comments that no one else would dare to voice.

At the end of the play, almost admitting that all his trickery was intentional, he asks the audience not to be 'offended' as all 'is mended'. His final lines imply that the play's premise is a 'weak and idle theme'. He suggests that the audience should treat it all as a dream. Reality and illusion continue to blur. It is interesting that in a play about power and control, Shakespeare gives the final lines to the servant and not to the master.

▼ Puck sending Helena to sleep at the end of Act 3.

Bottom

For many people, Bottom is the funniest and most memorable character in the play. He is magically transformed into an ass, and the queen of the fairies falls in love with him. The humour is generated partly by the situation Bottom finds himself in, partly by his lack of self-awareness and partly by the audience's recognition of his character and his faults. Through all his adventures, Bottom remains very human.

Bottom is pompous. In the 1999 film of *A Midsummer Night's Dream*, he was presented as a character who feels superior to his colleagues. He is fully involved in their play and its rehearsals and, although Quince is the director, Bottom has a tendency to take over: 'let me play Thisbe too. I'll speak in a monstrous little voice'. His self-belief, which is so misplaced, is also infectious and highlights his enthusiasm. His workmates do not appear to resent him, and welcome his reappearance with an ecstatic, 'O most courageous day! O most happy hour!' They are distraught when he goes missing and cannot conceive how they could perform their play without him: 'he hath simply the best wit of any handicraft man in Athens'. Their loyalty to him is endearing.

With the most wonderful irony, Puck places an ass's head on Bottom, making it clear what he thinks of this character. Bottom is the only mortal to have a relationship with a fairy, and this relationship is intriguing. Both Titania and Bottom are the victims of cruel magical tricks, and their brief 'love' affair is the result. When he wakes from his dream, the audience wonders if he has become a wiser man: 'I have had a dream, / past the wit of man to say what dream it was.' Here we see a very different Bottom: a thoughtful, articulate and reflective man.

Bottom is the only mortal character who has a role in all three plotlines. He is the Mechanicals' main actor, the lover of the enchanted fairy queen and the main performer for the newly married courtly couples. It is only his fellow labourers who truly appreciate him and his talents.

However, Shakespeare makes Bottom's performance as Pyramus as amateurish and as funny as the audience could wish, and some people's final impression is that he is still 'an ass'.

◆ **With a partner, consider how Shakespeare uses Bottom as a thematic linking device. Make notes on your ideas in response to the following questions:**

1. **How are the harshness of love, unrequited love and yearnings for the impossible explored through Bottom?**
2. **How does his character develop ideas on fantasy, dreams and magic?**
3. **How does Shakespeare investigate the fine line between ignorance and wisdom with Bottom?**

Quince

Peter Quince is the driving force for the rehearsal and production of the play to be performed at Theseus's wedding. He is the author of *The Most Lamentable Comedy and Most Cruel Death of Pyramus and Thisbe*. At the rehearsal in the wood, he takes on the role of director and is in charge of casting the play. He appears to know something about plays, how they are structured and meant to be performed and asserts to Flute: 'You speak all your part at once, cues and all.'

When performing the play, Quince recites the Prologue. It is an affecting scene as he struggles to fit his lines into the metre and make the rhymes work, with both comedic and tragic effect. The stage audience makes jokes at his expense.

Hermia

Hermia is a young woman at a time when a father had absolute authority over his daughter's choice of husband. Unfortunately, Hermia is in love with Lysander and her father is insisting that she marry Demetrius. Although she lacks real power, it is clear from the beginning that Hermia is willing to assert her views, taking centre stage to explain them: 'I would my father looked but with my eyes.' She is also willing to defy and humiliate her father publicly by agreeing to run away with Lysander.

Hermia is small – during the conflict Lysander calls her 'bead,' 'acorn' and 'dwarf' – but feisty. Hermia and Helena have enjoyed a close relationship since childhood, but their situation obviously puts a strain on the friendship. now Helena says of her:

O, when she is angry she is keen and shrewd;
She was a vixen when she went to school

Helena

Shakespeare presents Helena as a stark physical contrast to Hermia, who calls her a 'painted maypole' in their argument in Act 3. She is obviously tall and slim, and is usually cast as such.

We meet Helena at a low point in her life. She is very much in love with Demetrius, a young man who once courted her. He now wants to marry Hermia and has consequently rejected Helena. This has not altered her feelings, and she cannot understand his change of heart. She is conscious that there is something about Hermia that has attracted him:

O, teach me how you look, and with what art
You sway the motion of Demetrius' heart.

Although she makes much of the notion of sisterhood, 'Both warbling of one song, both in one key,' Helena is the only female in the play who is guilty of real disloyalty, with her disclosure to Demetrius of the elopement plan. Her pursuit of Demetrius when he is chasing another woman may seem undignified to a modern audience:

I am your spaniel; and, Demetrius,
The more you beat me I will fawn on you

Today, we sympathise with Helena as the victim of unrequited love, but might be doubtful about the way she copes with it. It is interesting that, although she achieves her happiness with Demetrius at the end, this only occurs after he is placed under the influence of Oberon's love potion. Is this a plot device or a comment on Helena's or Demetrius's character?

Lysander

Lysander is confident, despite the problems that he and Hermia face at the beginning. Certain of finding a way out of the situation and sure of Hermia's love, he is not undermined by Egeus's lack of support, Demetrius's competition or Theseus's initial decision.

Shakespeare presents Lysander as a proactive lover. He plans the elopement, but then loses his way in the wood. In some ways he is a stereotype: he tries hard to persuade Hermia to sleep with him, and when confronted with Demetrius's opposition he resorts to violence.

Demetrius

Demetrius appears much less likeable than Lysander. We never discover why Egeus prefers him. He does not say much in the first scene, but what he does say appears arrogant: 'Lysander, yield / Thy crazèd title to my certain right.' He seems rather careless of Hermia's lack of interest. Even less favourable is his rejection of Helena and his indifference to the hurt he has caused her. His behaviour to Helena in the woods is abusive and aggressive.

Egeus

Egeus's complaint against his daughter Hermia dominates the first scene. Shakespeare uses this character to introduce the themes of the law and control versus freedom. Egeus is determined to bring down the full force of the law on Hermia if she refuses to obey him. He seems to be motivated by a desire for control rather than by reason, and in the end Theseus denies his request.

Theseus and Hippolyta

Theseus and Hippolyta are the first two characters on the stage. Through them we are immediately introduced to the play's main themes of marriage, love and conflict: 'Now, fair Hippolyta, our nuptial hour / Draws on apace', 'Hippolyta, I wooed thee with my sword'.

These two characters and their story of war and wooing are based on Greek myth and have parallels with the fairy world. However, Hippolyta and Theseus never come into contact with the fairies and are more closely connected to the lovers through the exploration of sexual relationships.

Theseus has been played in various ways: as an autocratic politician, a lecherous rogue, a battle-weary young man and an elderly general. He is very much in charge in Act 1 Scene 1. It is problematic for an audience to make a judgement about a man who describes his own marriage and Hermia's death in the same short speech. Here, he wholly supports Egeus's demands, and yet a few days later he says 'Egeus, I will overbear your will'. Shakespeare does not make it clear what has caused this about-face. Perhaps Theseus has found himself moved by young love. Some productions show Hippolyta encouraging him towards this more feeling response.

Hippolyta only speaks twenty-eight lines in the play, and may appear passive: she makes no comment on the lovers' plight, leaving all the decision-making to Theseus. But Shakespeare presents her as a confident and thoughtful woman in Act 5. Here, she is willing to stand up to Theseus when discussing the lover's story, and offers her perspective.

Hippolyta comes from a tribe of powerful women, the Amazons. She has had to surrender to Theseus but he falls in love with her so, in effect, also surrenders to her.

◆ **In the production pictured here, Theseus and Hipployta are played by middle-aged actors. This would provide an interesting contrast with the much younger lovers. Make a list of the advantages and disadvantages of making the age difference so distinct. Consider which themes a director may wish to highlight by taking this approach.**

◆ In groups of four, each choose one of these characters: Theseus, Helena, Quince, Oberon. Prepare a PowerPoint presentation showing your personal reading of your chosen character, and present it to the other members of your group. Each presentation should include the following five slides:

- A picture of the actor that you would cast as your character in a new stage version of the play, with some bullet points to explain your rationale.
- Ideas on how this character should look on stage – their costume, hair and make-up. Consider the symbolism of your choices.
- The five most important quotations that reveal your character and their development. Include some language analysis.
- Some ideas on how this character is used by Shakespeare to move forward the plot and develop the play's themes.
- Your personal response to this character, with an explanation of how you think an audience would respond to them on stage.

The language of *A Midsummer Night's Dream*

Old language

Shakespeare's language may seem complex and difficult when you first encounter it. With experience it becomes easier, but it can still remain a challenge.

- **With a partner, choose a four-page section of the play. Then, working by yourself, divide the words explained on these pages into those that you can easily understand, those that you find difficult and those that seem to have no link with modern English. Afterwards, swap work with your partner so you can see how he or she has grouped these words. Discuss any differences, and try to explain words to each other if one of you finds them easier to understand.**

Of all the major writers in English, Shakespeare uses the largest number of different words: more than four times as many as most authors. He also uses many different meanings for the same words – he obviously enjoyed playing with language.

Shakespeare can also be hard to understand because today's world is so different from that of 400 years ago. Some speeches clearly display that difference, as in Act 2 Scene 1, lines 35–8:

That frights the maidens of the villagery,
Skim milk, and sometimes labour in the quern,
And bootless make the breathless housewife churn,
And sometime make the drink to bear no barm

Here, the agricultural England of the 1590s is much in evidence. However, there is little in the play that only a person from Shakespeare's time could understand.

Literary language

Shakespeare's language isn't just old, it's literary. *A Midsummer Night's Dream* draws upon many other types of writing and stories: Greek and Roman mythology, old plays and folk tales and legends. The language is also shaped for the Elizabethan stage. Unlike many of today's writers for film and television, Elizabethan playwrights often used complex and playful language rather than trying to be realistic.

People in Shakespeare's day did not speak like the characters in his plays; they certainly did not speak in rhyme! Shakespeare did not use the ordinary speech of real people – he followed the stage conventions of the time by writing much of the play in verse.

There are times when the language seems to run away with itself, as in Bottom's lines 205–7 in Act 4 Scene 1, where Shakespeare uses the Bible as his guide:

The eye of man hath not heard, the ear of man hath not seen, man's hand is not able to taste, his tongue to conceive, nor his heart to report what my dream was!

Shakespeare also uses **alliteration** to highlight the comedy implicit in the literary limitations of the Mechanicals:

Whereat with blade, with bloody, blameful blade,
He bravely broached his boiling bloody breast

- **Watch a TV drama and list some examples of when the dialogue mimics real speech. Do these moments have a distinct purpose – for example, to move the story on, or to reveal something about a character's past? Do any characters speak in a way that you never really hear in a conversation?**

Imagery

A Midsummer Night's Dream abounds in imagery (sometimes called 'figures' or 'figurative language'). Imagery is created by vivid words and phrases that conjure up emotionally charged mental pictures or associations in the imagination. Imagery provides insight into character or develops a theme, and stirs the audience's imagination. It also deepens the dramatic impact of particular moments.

Imagery works well when describing love. Lysander shows his love and concern when he says to Hermia:

How now, my love? Why is your cheek so pale?
How chance the roses there do fade so fast?

Helena, because of her unhappy situation, describes love as 'Cupid painted blind'. And at the end of the play, Demetrius describes his renewed love for Helena with an image that links love and health:

But like a sickness did I loathe this food.
But, as in health come to my natural taste

Problems in love and conflict are also described in terms of storms and bad weather. Hermia describes her tears as a 'tempest of my eyes', and Titania's 'forgeries of jealousy' speech (Act 2 Scene 1, lines 81–117) is filled with extreme images – 'contagious fogs', 'whistling wind' – that create a clear picture of a world in torment because of her 'wrath' with Oberon.

There is a predominance of natural imagery in the play. This is to some extent due to Shakespeare's presentation of the fairies, who are all named after things found in nature. The natural imagery also helps to link the woodland setting to the situations in which the characters find themselves. There was little scenery when the play was performed in Shakespeare's time so the language had to convey clearly the setting to the audience. When Puck torments the Mechanicals (Act 3 Scene 1, lines 89–93), he uses an abundance of frightening imagery so that the audience can picture the scene:

Through bog, through bush, through brake, through briar;
Sometime a horse I'll be, sometime a hound,
A hog, a headless bear, sometime a fire,
And neigh, and bark, and grunt, and roar, and burn,
Like horse, hound, hog, bear, fire at every turn.

A few lines later (103–6), Bottom responds with his own more comforting natural imagery to show he is not afraid:

The ousel cock so black of hue,
With orange-tawny bill,
The throstle with his note so true,
The wren with little quill –

Shakespeare uses the moon as a recurring image in the play, for a variety of effects. Theseus's image 'Chanting faint hymns to the cold fruitless moon' describes Hermia's life if she chooses to become a nun. Earlier, he uses the moon as a marker for the slow passing of time until his wedding day: 'how slow / This old moon wanes!' And in Act 1 Scene 1, lines 9–11, Hippolyta links the moon with night-time and dreams:

And then the moon, like to a silver bow
New bent in heaven, shall behold the night
Of our solemnities.

Most of the play takes place at night, and the language conjures up the image of a place with no light except moonlight, in which the characters stumble around, feeling vulnerable. The natural imagery highlights how the boundary between wisdom and foolishness has blurred. It is an excellent place to explore the complications of mortal love and the whims of human beings. The moon becomes a symbol of inconstancy and infidelity, highly relevant to Lysander's and Demetrius's fickleness. Lysander plans to meet Hermia under the light of the 'silver visage' of Phoebe (goddess of the moon, associated with chastity), but when in the wood standing on the grass decked 'with liquid pearl' he behaves in a less constant way.

The imagery of dreams and reality is fascinating and thought-provoking When she wakes up after her night in the wood (Act 4 Scene 1, lines 186–7), Hermia comments on the experience:

Methinks I see these things with parted eye,
When everything seems double.

Bottom is also puzzled by his memory of events and thinks it is 'past the wit of man to say what dream it was. Man is but an ass if he go about to expound this dream' (Act 4 Scene 1, lines 201–2). Bottom is trying to be philosophical and reflect upon the meaning of his vision, but his mixed-up imagery makes it even more confusing, and amusing for the audience. This is exactly what Oberon intended when he declared in Act 3 Scene 2, lines 370–1:

When they next wake, all this derision
Shall seem a dream and fruitless vision

The play is full of images of dreams. It ends with Theseus commenting on the Mechanicals' play: 'The best in this kind are but shadows; and the worst are no worse, if imagination amend them.' (Act 5 Scene 1, lines 205–6.) And at lines 403–6 Puck tells the audience to think:

That you have but slumbered here
While these visions did appear;
And this weak and idle theme,
No more yielding but a dream

The Mechanicals view the moon less as image or symbol. They want a physical representation of the moon in their play: a lantern. They cannot comprehend how language can create a moon, making it real for an audience.

Shakespeare's imagery uses metaphor, simile and personification. All are comparisons that substitute one thing (the image) for another (the thing that is actually being described).

A **simile** compares one thing to another, using 'as' or 'like'. Demetrius describes his love for Hermia, 'Melted as the snow'; and Lysander says he will shake Hermia from him 'like a serpent'. Earlier, Helena describes her friendship with Hermia as 'like to a double cherry'. Sometimes inappropriate similes can be used for comic effect. Thisbe, attempting romantic imagery, describes Pyramus: 'His eyes were green as leeks.'

A **metaphor** is also a comparison, suggesting that two dissimilar things are actually the same. A metaphor borrows one word or phrase to express another. In Act 3, when the lovers are in a potion-induced confusion, they use metaphor to put each other down. Lysander calls Hermia 'loathed medicine! O hated potion' and Hermia calls Helena a 'painted maypole'.

Personification is the attribution of human characteristics, such as personality, to non-human objects or abstract ideas.

Antithesis

LYSANDER *The course of true love never did run smooth;*
But either it was different in blood –
HERMIA *O cross! too high to be enthralled to low.*
LYSANDER *Or else misgraffed in respect of years –*
HERMIA *O spite! too old to be engaged to young.*
LYSANDER *Or else it stood upon the choice of friends –*
HERMIA *O hell, to choose love by another's eyes!*

The first of these lines from Act 1 Scene 1, lines 134–40, is now proverbial. The exclamations that follow ('O cross!' 'O spite!' 'O hell') are absurd and comical, but also highly patterned (notice the echoing rhythms of the last five lines). Shakespeare is using one of his favourite language devices, **antithesis** – setting words or phrases against each other to heighten the sense of conflict (high/low, old/young).

- **Try to find more examples of antithesis in moments like this, where the language seems to overwhelm or contradict the emotions.**
- **Consider again Shakespeare's use of binary opposition (introduced on p. 98). Look for one example in each act, and think about the effect on the audience at key moments in the play as the characters and themes unfold.**

Verse and prose

Although it has a good deal of rhyme, more of the play is written in **blank verse**: unrhymed verse with a five-beat rhythm (**iambic pentameter**). Each line has five **feet** (groups of syllables) called **iambs**, which have one stressed (/) and one unstressed (×) syllable:

× / × / × / × / × /
This man with lanthorn, dog, and bush of thorn

The court and the fairies mainly use this kind of verse, but (apart from their *Pyramus and Thisbe* play) the Mechanicals' speeches are in prose. Thus, the language of the characters reflects their social position as well as creating different types of comedy.

Shakespeare also uses other metres, most obviously four-stress rhythm – as in 'You spotted snakes with double tongue', and in the final sixty-seven lines of the play.

- **Write a modern speech in iambic pentameter. Try to imagine a scene that Shakespeare has omitted, such as a conversation between Helena and Hermia when they return to Athens.**

Language and character

The language of the characters – the words, patterns and images they use – reflects their personality as much as their actions or the plot do.

- ◆ Examine the speeches of your favourite character in order to identify the language patterns they use, and to what effect.
- ◆ Devise some dialogue that the actors could be speaking at the moment shown in the picture below. It can be in modern English or, if you want a real challenge, try to write dialogue in the style of Shakespeare himself!
- ◆ Create a poster that concentrates on the language of the play. Present some of the most important features of Shakespeare's language. Include some of the following ideas:
  - famous favourite lines from the play
  - examples of different kinds of wordplay and humour, with modern versions or interpretations
  - words and phrases no longer used today that you find interesting

  Display your ideas around the classroom. Look at each other's posters, and leave two comments on each: WWW (What Went Well) and EBI (Even Better If).

A Midsummer Night's Dream in performance

There is little clear evidence about when and where this play was originally performed. Shakespeare's earliest plays were performed at The Theatre, an open-air playhouse in Shoreditch, London. His company, The Chamberlain's Men, then moved their performances to the Globe Theatre. The theatre burnt down in 1613, and was rebuilt in 1997 as a copy of the original. The modern Shakespeare's Globe replicates to some extent the experience of Shakespeare's contemporaries, both as actors and audience.

When *A Midsummer Night's Dream* was first performed on stage, all the female parts were played by boys. This issue is amusingly explored through the character of Flute and his response to being cast as Thisbe: 'Nay, faith, let me not play a woman: I have a beard coming.'

There were few props and little in the way of sets. The audience had to imagine the contrast between the first scene in the palace and the night scenes in the wood. Most performances took place during the day. In this they were greatly helped by Shakespeare's imagery and the actors' responses.

- **Look at the picture below. What do you notice about the building, the staging and the audience in the modern Shakespeare's Globe? How is it different from other theatres you have attended? How might the audience experience differ?**

This 1900 production is in the lavish Victorian style, in which each scene resembles a living picture. The action of the play was in danger of becoming secondary to the setting.

The ways productions of *A Midsummer Night's Dream* have been staged over the years have to some extent been informed by changing social attitudes to marriage. For example, a Victorian audience may well have had a very different view from a modern one towards Hermia's refusal to yield to her father's wishes and her decision to elope with Lysander.

A production would also reflect the audience's perception of the whole notion of fairies, magic and the supernatural. Prior to Elizabethan times, fairies were considered to be evil. Shakespeare, along with other writers at the time, redefined fairies during this time period, turning them into gentle, albeit mischievous, spirits.

◀ **Northern Ballet Theatre's production of *A Midsummer Night's Dream*, 2007.**

Ballet and opera

A Midsummer Night's Dream has inspired ballets and operas. Operatic versions of Shakespeare's plays cut the language very heavily or rewrite it.

In 1692, Henry Purcell wrote the music for a spectacular operatic version called *The Fairy Queen*. David Garrick's operatic version, *The Fairies* (1755), dismissed all the characters except the lovers and the fairies. Fewer than 600 lines from Shakespeare's original remained, but there were an additional twenty-eight songs, some from other plays by Shakespeare and some from other poets, such as Dryden.

An opera with music by Benjamin Britten premiered in 1960. Britten connects his music to the three groups of characters. The Mechanicals are given folk-like 'simple' music, the lovers have a more romantic sound and a more ethereal music is used to represent the fairies. All of the action takes place in the woods and the fairies dominate, which is appropriate as Shakespeare associates them throughout with music and dancing. Britten focuses on the innocence and romanticism inherent in the lovers' story, rather than the sexuality. Puck is a naughty, acrobatic child.

All the action and characterisation in a ballet are interpreted through music and dance. George Balanchine choreographed a ballet version of the story using Mendelssohn's music written in 1843. The ballet tells the story in dance in two acts. The first act tells the story of the lovers and fairies, and the second focuses on a dancing marriage celebration. The ballet was first performed in 1962.

Music and dance have always played a large part in productions of the play, and continue to do so. Directors often commission composers to write original scores for new productions.

- **In groups of four, compose a short piece of music and choreograph a dance sequence for Act 4 Scene 1, from line 80 ('*Soft music plays*') and line 83 ('*They dance*') up to line 99 ('*Exeunt Oberon, Titania and Puck*'). Try out your ideas and show the result to another group.**

▶ **Oberon and Puck enter the stage from above in Peter Brook's 1970 production of the play.**

Modern productions

In contrast to the lavish productions and the focus on dance and musical set pieces so beloved of Victorian audiences, Peter Brook's production of the play in 1970 presented a radical new interpretation. The stage was spartan, the set a stark white box, the costumes simple and in primary colours. The fairies were shown suspended above the stage on trapeze-like swings and were lowered up and down for their interactions with the mortals. The magic in the play was interpreted through circus tricks and acrobatics. Many of the relationships were presented in crudely sexual terms. It proved to be an influential production, and many companies, directors and costume and set designers have imitated these ideas and developed them further in the last forty years.

▼ **This Korean production used music, movement-based acting, mythology and mime to create a fun and energetic interpretation of the play.**

Shakespeare is often thought of as English through and through, and *A Midsummer Night's Dream* particularly so, yet successful and well-received productions take place all over the world.

Tim Supple directed a successful production using dancers, martial arts experts, musicians and street acrobats from across India and Sri Lanka to reproduce the mysterious and surreal world of the fairies. The production toured India to great acclaim, and had a successful run at the Swan Theatre in Stratford-upon-Avon in 2007 and 2008. It used traditional live Indian music, bright and beautiful costumes and was performed in six Indian languages and English. *The Times* newspaper described this production as 'Shakespeare brilliantly reimagined'. There are other photographs of this production on pages 44 and 50.

▼ The fairies tumbling down acrobatically in Tim Supple's vision of *A Midsummer Night's Dream*.

Presentations of the fairy world

Titania and her fairies have been presented in many different ways. The photograph below is of a 2001 production. It shows Titania surrounded by her fairies, who are presented as childlike creatures.

In contrast, the image on the right, from a 1992 National Theatre production, shows a very different Titania. Here, the imagery is much darker and more sinister. Bottom appears as the captive of the fairies, who look like they have emerged from the underworld.

- **Compile a list of the dramatic gains and losses of presenting the fairies as these two productions have. Which do you prefer? Why?**

A 2001 production had an all-female cast playing the Mechanicals. The comedian and writer Dawn French played Bottom. This gender role-reversal is the opposite of that in Shakespeare's day, when all the characters – including the female ones – were played by men or boys.

- **In a group, discuss the considerations you think influenced this casting decision and the effects it might have had on characterisation and the development of the relationships on stage. What challenges might it present to the actors involved? How are they similar or different to the challenges for an all-male cast playing both genders in Elizabethan theatre productions?**

▶ 'Let me play the lion too. I will roar'.

Set design

No Shakespearean comedy offers wider scope to the imagination of directors, designers, and actors.

(David Richman, *Laughter, Pain, and Wonder: Shakespeare's Comedies and the Audience in the Theatre*, 1990)

This play is indeed a set designer's 'dream'. It includes a duke's palace and the magical world of fairies, all contrasted with a group of unworldly and comical amateur dramatics. Much of the action takes place at night, and the imagery encourages a creative response to Shakespeare's vision.

When studying or acting in a Shakespeare play, one question always arises: 'What does it all mean?' The answer is that it means different things at different times and also many things at once. *A Midsummer Night's Dream* has been acted for over 400 years and people are still debating and exploring its different meanings and interpretations. The complexity of the play and its language is part of its appeal. It is an exploration in which there is no final, complete and 'right' explanation. Perhaps Bottom was right:

I have had a most rare vision. I have had a dream, past the wit of man to say what dream it was.

- **The striking school setting shown on this page will have been the combined vision of a director, a set designer and a lighting designer. In threes, each taking one of these roles, combine your ideas to create your own vision of a key moment in the play.**
- **As much of its action takes place in the woods at night, *A Midsummer Night's Dream* is popular for outdoor evening productions, often in parks or country house gardens. What type of outdoor space would you consider using, and which aspects of the play would it enhance?**

Writing about Shakespeare

The play as text

Shakespeare's plays have always been studied as literary works – as words on a page that need clarification, appreciation and discussion. When you write about the plays, you will be asked to compose short pieces and also longer, more reflective pieces like controlled assessments, examination scripts and coursework – often in the form of essays on themes and/or imagery, character studies, analyses of the structure of the play and on stagecraft. Imagery, stagecraft and character are dealt with elsewhere in this edition. Here, we concentrate on themes and structure. You might find it helpful to look at the 'Write about it' boxes on the left-hand pages throughout the play.

Themes

It is often tempting to say that the theme of a play is a single idea, like 'death' in *Hamlet*, or 'the supernatural' in *Macbeth*, or 'love' in *Romeo and Juliet*. The problem with such a simple approach is that you will miss the complexity of the plays. In *Romeo and Juliet*, for example, the play is about the relationship between love, family loyalty and constraint; it is also about the relationship of youth to age and experience; and the relationship between Romeo and Juliet is also played out against a background of enmity between two families. Between each of these ideas or concepts there are tensions. The tensions are the main focus of attention for Shakespeare and the audience, and they also happen to be how drama operates – by the presentation of and resolution of tension.

Look back at the 'Themes' boxes throughout the play to see if any of the activities there have given rise to information that you could use as a starting-point for further writing about the themes of the specific play you are studying.

Structure

Most Shakespeare plays are in five acts, divided into scenes. These acts were not in the original scripts, but have been included in later editions to make the action more manageable, clearer and more like 'classical' structures. One way to get a sense of the structure of the whole play is to take a printed version of the play (not this one!) and cut it up into scenes and acts. Then display each scene and act, in sequence, on a wall, like this:

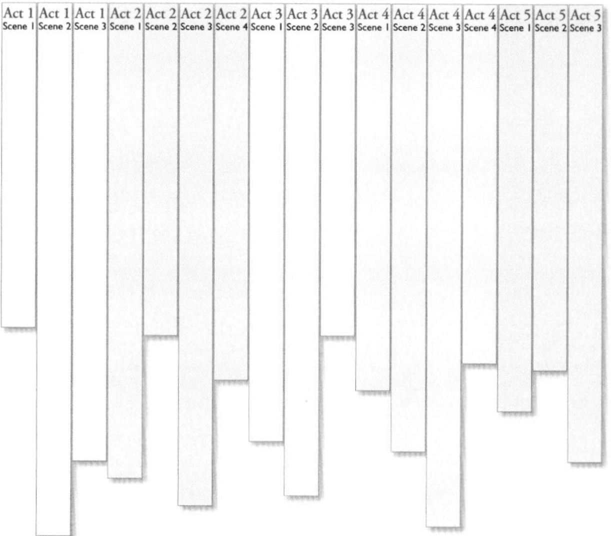

As you set out the whole play, you will be able to see the 'shape' of each act, the relative length of the scenes, and how the acts relate to each other (such as whether one of the acts is shorter, and why that might be). You can annotate the text with comments, observations and questions. You can use a highlighter pen to mark the recurrence of certain words, images or metaphors to see at a glance where and how frequently they appear. You can also follow a particular character's progress through the play.

Such an overview of the play gives you critical perspective: you will be able to see how the parts fit together, to stand back from the play and assess its shape, and to focus on particular parts within the context of the whole. Your writing will reflect a greater awareness of the overall context as a result.

The play as script

There are different, but related, categories when we think of the play as a script for performance. These include *stagecraft* (discussed elsewhere in this edition and throughout the left-hand pages), *lighting*, *focus* (who are we looking at? Where is the attention of the audience?), *music and sound*, *props and costumes*, *casting*, *make-up*, *pace and rhythm*, and other *spatial relationships* (e.g. how actors move across stage in relation to each other). If you are writing about stagecraft or performance, use the notes you have made as a result of the 'Stagecraft' boxes throughout this edition of the play, as well as any material you can gather about the plays in performance.

What are the key points of dispute?

Shakespeare is brilliant at capturing a number of key points of dispute in each of his plays. These are the dramatic moments where he concentrates the focus of the audience on difficult (sometimes universal) problems that the characters are facing or embodying.

First, identify these key points in the play you are studying. You can do this as a class by brainstorming what you think the key points are in small groups, then debating the long-list as a whole class, and then coming up with a short-list of what the class thinks are the most significant. (This is a good opportunity for speaking and listening work.) They are likely to be places in the play where the action or reflection is at its most intense, and which capture the complexity of themes, character, structure and performance.

Second, drill down at one of the points of contention and tension. In other words, investigate the complexity of the problem that Shakespeare is exploring. What is at stake? Why is it important? Is it a problem that can be resolved, or is it an insoluble one?

Key skills in writing about Shakespeare

Here are some suggestions to help you organise your notes and develop advanced writing skills when working on Shakespeare:

- Compose the title of your writing carefully to maximise your opportunities to be creative and critical about the play; or explore the key words in your title carefully. Decide which aspect of the play – or which combination of aspects – you are focusing on.
- Create a mind map of your ideas, making connections between them.
- If appropriate, arrange your ideas into a hierarchy that shows how some themes or features of the play are 'higher' than others and can incorporate other ideas.
- Sequence your ideas so that you have a plan for writing an essay, review, story – whichever genre you are using. You might like to think about whether to put your strongest points first, in the middle, or later.
- Collect key quotations (it might help to compile this list with a partner), which you can use as evidence to support your argument.
- Compose your first draft, embedding quotations in your text as you go along.
- Revise your draft in the light of your own critical reflections and/or those of others.

The following pages focus on writing about *A Midsummer Night's Dream* in particular.

Writing about *A Midsummer Night's Dream*

Before embarking on an extended piece of writing, it is important to think carefully about how it is structured. This play is a comedy and complies with the comic conventions of Elizabethan theatre. The plot is typically arranged into five acts, with an accepted formula:

Act 1 A situation with tensions or conflict
Act 2 Conflict is developed
Act 3 Conflict reaches a climax and often an impasse
Act 4 Problem or conflict begins to be sorted out
Act 5 Problem is resolved and loose ends are tied up

- With a partner, look at each act and consider:
  - the development of the main characters and the outcome for each one
  - how the main themes are developed and how and when each is concluded
  - how Shakespeare introduces and develops the imagery
  - the tone and mood, for example the moments of dramatic tension, empathy, humour and happiness.

Extended writing on a Shakespeare play is a challenge. It is important that you have had the opportunity to develop a personal response. The next two activities test your ideas, help you to build your argument and see how you can you use the text to support it.

- In groups of four, take one question each and write down your ideas in full, using quotations to support your ideas:
  - What is the turning point in the play?
  - What is the most memorable moment?
  - Which is the most important line?
  - Who is the most important character?

- In turn, take one minute to explain your ideas to your group. As the others in your group are speaking, make notes of their ideas and write down questions. Don't let each other off lightly; ask your questions so that each individual has to explain their response and justify it with quotations.

- In pairs, consider the following readings of the play. Divide them into three categories: Yes (those you agree with), No (those you don't agree with) and Maybe (those you are not sure about). It is very important that any argument you construct is supported by appropriate quotations. Share your responses with another pair.

1 Shakespeare is presenting men as fickle and women as constant and true.
2 Shakespeare believes that the patriarchal society must not be changed. Men must make all the decisions.
3 Shakespeare presents love as involving more suffering than pleasure; more of a nightmare than a dream.
4 Shakespeare believes that love will not last forever and will always change.
5 Shakespeare thinks that true love is beautiful and the imagery in this play is evidence of this.
6 Conflict in the play is the more dominant theme. Romance is secondary. This is a dark play where we are laughing at the characters.
7 The tone of the play is so light-hearted that the audience never doubts that things will end happily, and is therefore free to enjoy the comedy without being caught up in the tension of an uncertain outcome.
8 Shakespeare is interested in imbalance in relationships; he enjoys exploring unrequited love and arguments.

Essays

You may have some choice in your essay title for *A Midsummer Night's Dream*. However, it is likely that coursework, controlled assessment or exam practice essay titles will be suggested to you. The best essay titles are those that encourage you to formulate a line of argument. A quotation or statement can be useful starting points. For example:

Sigmund Freud said: 'You are always insane when you are in love.' Analyse this statement in relation to Shakespeare's presentation of the lovers in Act 4 Scene 2 of A Midsummer Night's Dream.

'Helena is presented by Shakespeare as a desperate character with whom the audience has little sympathy.' Analyse the presentation of this important character in light of this statement.

It is better to focus on a precise area of the play – for example, the interactions in one particular scene, the presentation of a character, the development of a theme or Shakespeare's use of imagery and its impact on the audience. This tight focus allows for a more thoughtful and profound exploration.

Structuring your essay

The introduction needs to fulfil two main functions: to address the question, and to launch the line of argument you will construct in response to the question.

First impressions count, and you will need to leave your reader keen to find out how you develop the ideas you have introduced. If this is an examination essay, your assessor will, from the first sentence, be judging your skills and evaluating how well you are addressing the assessment objectives.

Just as Shakespeare has structured his play into acts, you will need to structure your ideas into paragraphs, so that your reader experiences your essay as a journey. Each paragraph will explore a particular focus or analyse an idea. The first sentence of each paragraph, sometimes called a topic sentence, is important. At the end of your first draft, reread all your topic sentences. They should stand alone as an outline of your argument and give a direction to your work. A useful analogy is to think of these opening sentences as the skeleton of your essay, with the development, textual support and analysis as the flesh, or meat, of the essay.

- Consider how you would answer the following essay questions. Which one would you like to write most and which least? Which would allow you to show your skills and ideas?

  1 Explore Shakespeare's use of setting in *A Midsummer Night's Dream*. Focus particularly on the opening scenes in Athens and the move to the woods at night for Acts 2, 3 and 4. What effect do these scenes have on the development of themes and character?

  2 Lysander's line, 'The course of true love never did run smooth', is one of the most famous in the play. Analyse how Shakespeare presents love in Act 1 Scene 1 of *A Midsummer Night's Dream*.

  3 How does Shakespeare use language in Act 3 Scene 2 to explore love and hate?

  4 Consider the ways that Shakespeare explores the ideas of dreams and reality in Act 4.

  5 'Oberon is a dangerous character using illusion and magic purely for control.' Respond to this statement by analysing Shakespeare's presentation of Oberon in *A Midsummer Night's Dream*.

  6 Explore the way that the play *Pyramus and Thisbe* is presented. What themes and ideas are explored by the dramatic device of a play within a play?

- Plan a response to two of these titles. Then choose one of them to research further and draft into an essay.

William Shakespeare 1564–1616

1564 Born Stratford-upon-Avon, eldest son of John and Mary Shakespeare.
1582 Marries Anne Hathaway of Shottery, near Stratford.
1583 Daughter Susanna born.
1585 Twins, son and daughter, Hamnet and Judith, born.
1592 First mention of Shakespeare in London. Robert Greene, another playwright, described Shakespeare as 'an upstart crow beautified with our feathers'. Greene seems to have been jealous of Shakespeare. He mocked Shakespeare's name, calling him 'the only Shake-scene in a country' (presumably because Shakespeare was writing successful plays).
1595 Becomes a shareholder in The Lord Chamberlain's Men, an acting company that became extremely popular.
1596 Son, Hamnet, dies, aged eleven.
Father, John, granted arms (acknowledged as a gentleman).
1597 Buys New Place, the grandest house in Stratford.
1598 Acts in Ben Jonson's *Every Man in His Humour.*
1599 Globe Theatre opens on Bankside. Performances in the open air.
1601 Father, John, dies.
1603 James I grants Shakespeare's company a royal patent: The Lord Chamberlain's Men become The King's Men and play about twelve performances each year at court.
1607 Daughter Susanna marries Dr John Hall.
1608 Mother, Mary, dies.
1609 The King's Men begin performing indoors at Blackfriars Theatre.
1610 Probably returns from London to live in Stratford.
1616 Daughter Judith marries Thomas Quiney.
Dies. Buried in Holy Trinity Church, Stratford-upon-Avon.

The plays and poems

(no one knows exactly when he wrote each play)

1589–95 *The Two Gentlemen of Verona, The Taming of the Shrew, First, Second* and *Third Parts* of *King Henry VI, Titus Andronicus, King Richard III, The Comedy of Errors, Love's Labour's Lost,* ***A Midsummer Night's Dream****, Romeo and Juliet, King Richard II* (and the long poems *Venus and Adonis* and *The Rape of Lucrece*).
1596–9 *King John, The Merchant of Venice, First* and *Second Parts* of *King Henry IV, The Merry Wives of Windsor, Much Ado About Nothing, King Henry V, Julius Caesar* (and probably the Sonnets).
1600–5 *As You Like It, Hamlet, Twelfth Night, Troilus and Cressida, Measure for Measure, Othello, All's Well That Ends Well, Timon of Athens, King Lear.*
1606–11 *Macbeth, Antony and Cleopatra, Pericles, Coriolanus, The Winter's Tale, Cymbeline, The Tempest.*
1613 *King Henry VIII, The Two Noble Kinsmen* (both probably with John Fletcher).
1623 Shakespeare's plays published as a collection (now called the First Folio).

Acknowledgements

Cambridge University Press would like to acknowledge the contributions made to this work by Rex Gibson.

Picture Credits

p. iii: Chichester Festival Theatre 2004, © Donald Cooper/ Photostage; p. v top: Royal Shakespeare Theatre 1999, © Donald Cooper/Photostage; p. v bottom: Chichester Festival Theatre 2004, © Donald Cooper/Photostage; p. vi: Royal Shakespeare Theatre 2005, © Donald Cooper/ Photostage; p. vii top: Royal Shakespeare Theatre 1958, © Getty Images; p. vii bottom: Ludlow Festival 2006, © Donald Cooper/Photostage; p. viii left: Royal Shakespeare Theatre 2002, © Donald Cooper/Photostage; p. viii top right: Royal Shakespeare Theatre 2005, © Donald Cooper/ Photostage; p. viii bottom right: Crucible Theatre 2003, © Donald Cooper/Photostage; p. ix top: Shakespeare's Globe 2008, © Sheila Burnett/ArenaPAL; p. ix bottom: National Theatre 2002, © Donald Cooper/Photostage; p. x top: Barbican Theatre 1995, © Donald Cooper/Photostage; p. x bottom: Chicago Shakespeare Theater 2012, © Liz Lauren; p. xi top: Open Air Theatre Regent's Park 2012, © Marilyn Kingwill/ArenaPAL; p. xi bottom: still from 1999 *A Midsummer Night's Dream* movie, dir: Michael Hoffman, © 20th Century Fox/The Kobal Collection/Mario Tursi; p. xii top: Ludlow Festival 2006, © Donald Cooper/ Photostage; p. xii bottom: Royal Shakespeare Theatre 2011, © Geraint Lewis; p. 4: Chichester Festival Theatre 2004, © Donald Cooper/Photostage; p. 12: Royal Shakespeare Theatre 1994, © Clive Barda/ArenaPAL; p. 16 'Cupid's Arrows' by Léon Bazile Perrault, Wikimedia; p. 18: Open Air Theatre Regent's Park 2004, © Donald Cooper/ Photostage; p. 22: Ludlow Festival 2006, © Donald Cooper/ Photostage; p. 24: Stratford Shakespeare Festival, Ontario 1977, © Zoë Dominic; p. 25: Shakespeare's Globe 2002, © Geraint Lewis; p. 28 'Cottingley Fairies' photograph, © National Museum of Photography, Film & Television/ Science & Society Picture Library; p. 30: Royal Shakespeare Theatre 1999, © Donald Cooper/Photostage; p. 34: still from 1999 *A Midsummer Night's Dream* movie. dir: Michael Hoffman, © 20th Century Fox/The Kobal Collection/Mario Tursi; p. 40: Ludlow Festival 2006, © Donald Cooper/ Photostage; p. 42 top: Britten Leeds Grand Theatre, Opera North 2008, © Clive Barda/ArenaPAL; p. 42 bottom: © Dreamstime, Goce; p. 44: Roundhouse 2007, © Geraint Lewis; p. 48 © Fine Art Photographic Library/Corbis; p. 50: Roundhouse 2007, © Donald Cooper/Photostage; p. 52: Ludlow Festival 2006, © Donald Cooper/Photostage; p. 54–55: © Robbie Jack/Corbis; p. 55: Illustration from 1628 book *Robin Goodfellow: His Mad Pranks and Merry Jests*, 1628 © Mary Evans/J. Bedmar/Iberfoto; p. 56: Royal Shakespeare Theatre 2002, © Donald Cooper/Photostage; p. 58: Ludlow Festival 2006, © Donald Cooper/Photostage; p. 60: Britten Leeds Grand Theatre, Opera North 2008, © Clive Barda/ ArenaPAL; p. 62: Open Air Theatre Regent's Park 2004, © Geraint Lewis; p. 64: Ludlow Festival 2006, © Donald Cooper/Photostage; p. 66: Royal Shakespeare Theatre 1989, © Donald Cooper/Photostage; p. 68: Courtyard Theatre 2008, © Donald Cooper/Photostage; p. 70: Open Air Theatre Regent's Park 2004, © Johan Persson/ArenaPAL; p. 74 'Puck' by Sir Joshua Reynolds, 1789, © Bridgeman Art Library; p. 76: Ludlow Festival 2006, © Donald Cooper/Photostage; p. 78: Barbican Theatre 1995, © Donald Cooper/Photostage; p. 80: Novello Theatre 2009, © Donald Cooper/Photostage; p. 82: Royal Shakespeare Theatre 2011, © Ellie Kurtz/ Royal Shakespeare Company; p. 84: Royal Shakespeare Theatre 2005, © Geraint Lewis; p. 86: Royal Shakespeare Theatre 2005, © Geraint Lewis; p. 88 Royal Shakespeare Theatre 2002, © Donald Cooper/Photostage; p. 90: Royal Shakespeare Theatre 2011, © Geraint Lewis; p. 92: Salzburg Festival 2007, © AFP/Getty Images; p. 94: Willamette University Theater 2008, © Chris L. Harris; p. 96: Royal Shakespeare Theatre 2011, © Geraint Lewis; p. 99: 'The Nightmare' by John Henry Fuseli, 1781, Wikimedia; p. 100: Ludlow Festival 2006, © Donald Cooper/Photostage; p. 102: Rose Theatre, Kingston 2010, © Nobby Clark/ ArenaPAL; p. 104: Open Air Theatre Regent's Park 2006, © Donald Cooper/Photostage; p. 114: Intiman Theatre 2011, © John Ulman; p. 116: Open Air Theatre Regent's Park 2006, © Marilyn Kingwill/ArenaPAL; p. 118: Open Air Theatre Regent's Park 2012, © Marilyn Kingwill/ArenaPAL;

p. 120: Great River Shakespeare Festival 2004, © Alec Wild; p. 126: Royal Shakespeare Theatre 2005, © Donald Cooper/Photostage; p. 130 top: Barbican Theatre 1995, © Donald Cooper/Photostage; p. 130 bottom: The Roundhouse 2007, © Donald Cooper/Photostage; p. 132: Watermill Theatre, Berkshire 2003, © Colin Willoughby/ArenaPAL; p. 134: Opera London 1990, © Clive Barda/ArenaPAL; p. 136: *Romeo and Juliet*, Royal Opera 2000, © Donald Cooper/Photostage; p. 138: Ludlow Festival 2006, © Donald Cooper/Photostage; p. 140: Brookside Theater, New Hampshire, USA, © Waterville Valley, NH/Shakespeare in the Valley; p. 142: Barbican Theatre 1989, © Donald Cooper/Photostage; p. 144: Barbican Theatre 1987, © Donald Cooper/Photostage; p. 146: Chichester Festival Theatre 2004, © Donald Cooper/Photostage; p. 148: Courtyard Theatre 2008, © Nigel Norrington/ArenaPAL; p. 149: Linbury Studio Theatre 2005, © Johan Persson/ArenaPAL; p. 156: Glyndebourne Festival 2006, © Donald Cooper/Photostage; p. 157: Chichester Festival Theatre 2004, © Donald Cooper/Photostage; p. 158: Glyndebourne Festival 2006, © Donald Cooper/Photostage; p. 161: Chichester Festival Theatre 2004, © Donald Cooper/Photostage; p. 165: Shakespeare's Globe 2002, © Donald Cooper/Photostage; p. 166: *Richard III*, Shakespeare's Globe 2012, © Franz-Marc Frei/Corbis; p. 167: 1900, His Majesty's Theatre, © V&A Images; p. 168: Northern Ballet Theatre 2008, © Merlin Hendy; p. 169 bottom: Arts Centre Melbourne, 2010, © AFP/Getty Images; p. 169 top: Royal Shakespeare Theatre 1970, © Donald Cooper/Photostage; p. 170: Roundhouse 2007, © Donald Cooper/Photostage; p. 171: National Theatre 1992, © Donald Cooper/Photostage; p. 172: Alberry Theatre 2001, © Donald Cooper/Photostage; p. 173 bottom: London Coliseum 2011, © Sisi Burn/ArenaPAL; p. 173 top: Open Air Theatre Regent's Park 2012, © Marilyn Kingwill/ArenaPAL.

Produced for Cambridge University Press by
White-Thomson Publishing
+44 (0)843 208 7460
www.wtpub.co.uk

Project editor: Alice Harman
Designer: Clare Nicholas
Concept design: Jackie Hill